The Power of Pivoting

How to Embrace Change and Create a Life You Love

MONIC

Monica Ortega

The Power of Pivoting
How to Embrace Change and Create a Life You
Love

Published by Monica Ortega
www.powerofpivoting.com

The author of this book does not provide any
medical advice or prescribe any of the
techniques discussed in this book as a form of
treatment without the advice of a licensed
physician. The author only intends to offer
general information based on her own
experiences. The author and publisher assume
no responsibility for any actions taken based on
the content herein.

Discounted rates are available for books bought
in bulk for sales promotion or corporate use.
Special editions or signed copies can be arranged
when purchased in bulk. For assistance in
ordering contact powerofpivoting@gmail.com.

ISBN: 978-0-578-86275-0

E-book ISBN: 978-0-578-86276-7

Copyright: TXu002237724

Cover Design: Jelena Mirkovic

Editing: Jackie Rapetti and Carole Ortega

Interior Design: Rik – Wild Seas Formatting

For more information or bulk ordering go to
www.powerofpivoting.com

To connect with Monica, follow her travel show *Monica Goes*, and learn more about The Power of Pivoting, scan the QR code below or visit www.monicagoes.com and sign up for the newsletter.

Dedication

This book is dedicated to all of the lost and broken souls finding themselves in the middle of a pivot who need to hear "It's ok to not be ok."

To those who were in my life, just doing the best they could with what they knew, thank you for the lessons.

And, of course, to my friends, family, and loved ones (old and new) who have stood by my side through it all! Y'all are freaking rockstars!

Contents

Introduction

Four years ago, my life did a complete 180 overnight. The ultimate pivot, for me, came when I found out that my then-husband had been cheating on me. While I was shocked and devastated, I had also spent the past few years living as a depressed shell of a person in an unhappy and emotionally abusive marriage. So when he finally came clean about his infidelity, it was as if a massive weight had lifted off my shoulders. I was free! I could start over! I got another chance! Within three days of finding out, I had a new place to live and the divorce papers written up. But more on that story later…

Pivoting is a natural part of life. Change is inevitable. We see it when relationships end (and when they begin), careers change, money and friends come and go, and sometimes the entire world shifts (oh hey, 2020!). The key is to expect the unexpected, learn to lean into the pivot, prepare for the side effects and emotional baggage, and start using those setbacks as set-ups.

For a long time I defined my "second chance" as my life post-divorce, but I've realized that, like everyone, my life has been constantly changing and shifting since the day that I was born. In this book I'll take you through some of the biggest changes and shifts in my life and the lessons I've learned along the way.

We'll break down tips and tools to help you make the best of these crazy times, and set up a plan to turn your next pivot into unimaginable success!

To kick things off, I'll leave (or start) you with my favorite quote from the movie "Hope Floats."

"Beginnings are scary, endings are usually sad, but it's the middle that counts. Remember that when you find yourself at the beginning."

~ Hope Floats

Chapter One:
The Oh-So-Scary Changes

So much of who we are as adults and how we function day-to-day is a product of our childhood and how we were raised (thanks, mom and dad!) The key, with anything really, is to take the good stuff and make them habits and take the bad stuff and learn from the lessons. Right out of the gate we are taught that change is scary.

Reinvention vs. Becoming Who We Really Are

When I was ten years old my parents moved our family from the inner city of Lansing, Michigan to the suburbs and I got my first real dose of change. As a young impressionable girl whose main goal in life at the time was to "be cool" and well-liked, this meant a reinvention. I went from wearing oversized Starter jackets and swearing with the mean girls, to realizing – seemingly overnight – that this just wouldn't work in suburbia. I quickly became the class clown, started joining sports teams, and soon became a cheerleader. We'll call these my "chameleon years."

I even changed my name! Growing up my parents called me by my nickname Niki. But after a really cool new girl named Monica moved to town, and a really mean girl named Niki started in with her shenanigans, I decided to start going by my legal name: Monica. There was even an awkward year when I tried to be even MORE cool, and changed the spelling to "Monika" (it didn't stick).

The point being, so much of it, at that age, comes down to how we fit in (or don't) with our peers at school. Before we learn the art of the pivot, it's all about reinvention. The bonus to these awkward years is that we learn a lot about what we like, and don't like, by trying lots of different things. We've all had those awkward phases of trying out new fashion styles. It turns out pleather pants and leopard print was NOT a good look...weird!

Developing Comfort Zones

So often, out of pure love and protection, our parents try to shield us from change. Right out of the gate, we're taught that change is scary. As kids, we're born fearless, ready to dive in and try it all. But over time we begin to develop comfort zones; the places we feel the safest where it's least likely for bad things (aka changes) to happen. I am also a product of the generation cusp between

Generation X and Generation Z or, as comedian Iliza Shlesinger refers to us, an "elder millennial." This means that our grandparents grew up in the depression era, learning to hoard everything and play it VERY safe. They then taught our parents to get steady jobs and, while yes chase your dreams, be sure to provide for your family. Our parents, having mostly what they needed, then taught us to "shoot for the moon!" and "anything is possible!" But also "be careful!" and "change is scary!" Very mixed messaging. In turn, I learned to dream big…but fear everything!

When changes started occurring in my life, I wasn't equipped to see them as opportunities quite yet. All I knew was to fit in and do my best. This fear of change later turned into a PLAN EVERYTHING mentality to try to control every outcome of my life. Well, that kind of thinking turns into a LOT of anxiety and, as we know, our plans rarely work out the way we expect them to.

Breaking Out of Your Comfort Zones

By the time we turn 30, we've concocted a whole slew of things in our minds that could possibly go wrong. We begin to develop our comfort zones and while safe and cozy, many of us get stuck there and call it a day. We may think, "I'm scared of heights, so I guess I'm not ever going to be an outdoorsy person" or "This job pays the bills and I never want to be broke, so I guess I'll stay here" or "I'm not happy in this relationship, but I guess it's better than nothing." Yikes!

When we start making compromises, we set ourselves up for a boring ho-hum kind of life...and where's the fun in that?! We only get one of these, so why not really go for it and have fun with the crazy things that develop along the way? I'm a big fan of failing forward.

The same way that it's important to figure out your motivation for becoming who you are (and who you want to be), it's equally as important to really dig in and find out what your comfort zones are ACTUALLY protecting you from. Is your fear of heights REALLY keeping you inside?

Is there a middle-ground-kind-of-hike you can try out to see if you like it? Or is it something else like, "I don't want to go alone" or "I don't see myself as an outdoorsy person." What if, what if, what if...we can always find a million reasons NOT to do something. But what if you just tried?

I have this theory: in life, you should try everything TWICE! Why twice? Because the first time we do something we tend to color the experience with our preconceived opinions and go into it a little jaded. "Oooh I just KNOW I'm going to hate squid, it SOUNDS disgusting!" Before we've even tried something, we've decided how we're going to feel about it. And because our brains are oh-so-happy to oblige with what we've already convinced them is a fact – surprise, surprise – you find squid disgusting. But maybe, just maybe, if you try it a second time with a more open mind you may feel differently.

I've applied this theory to nearly everything I've tried in life; usually it's a weird food or adventure. I'm afraid of almost EVERYTHING (which is why I became an adventure travel host, obviously) so, to really put my fears to the test, I try it all. I've gone on some adventures that I just KNEW I'd hate (white water rafting) and then was quite happily proven wrong and have gone back time and time again. The "try it twice" rule doesn't always change your mind though, and that's ok too.

At least you know you really don't like something and it's not just a preconceived bias you had. There are certain hikes where I've said, "Cool. Crossed it off the bucket list, I'm GOOD!" Or, as I always tell people, "Try everything twice... except for haggis (if you know what that is, you get it)..." But even that, in reality, I'd give another go!

Life is a bit of a trial and error game. From the time we're born, our brains start putting together who we are, what we like, and who we want to become. As you try different things (hopefully TWICE), your brain starts to develop a mental list of what's "good" and what's "bad." Adding more good things that we like to our lives boosts our overall happiness and puts us on a track to living a life we love. And as we start to figure out bad things we don't like, we become aware of which roads to avoid.

It's like in school when we were forced to take multiple subjects. Maybe you thought, "Oh hey, English is pretty cool and I don't totally suck at it!" That, in turn, had you thinking of careers where you could keep doing more of this thing you didn't totally suck at – and even get paid for it! When something triggers those good feelings, make a mental note of it (or better yet, take an actual pen to paper and write it down!), and find ways to add more of those positively stimulating actions into your life. In with the good, out with the bad.

Questioning Your Comfort Zones

Ask yourself this question: is your comfort zone REALLY protecting you from going broke? Or is it holding you back from doing the things you actually want to be doing? Is there a way that you can create a plan to do both? Save up AND find a new job you actually love? Who knows, it may even pay more! And the fact is, when we're happy in life we attract more abundance into our lives. What may seem like an irresponsible financial choice may also bring about more wealth in the long run.

Is being in an unhappy relationship REALLY better than being single? What if the person of your dreams is right around the corner just waiting for you to dump your loser boyfriend, sweep you off your feet, and show you what real love looks like? What if you step out single and, God-forbid, you're on your own for a long time and ACTUALLY start to love who you are? You may finally get to do the things you've always wanted to do without having someone who drags you down. What a wild concept!

Of course, some comfort zones are good and healthy. No, I don't want to jump off the side of a cliff in a wing-suit. I'm totally ok staying alive, thanks! But it's natural for people to use certain comfort zones as a crutch to "protect themselves" and to avoid dealing with the reality of the situation. Maybe you're just afraid. And while it's ok to be scared, ask yourself, "What am I really gaining from this fear? Is it leading me toward, or away, from the badass life I truly desire?"

Our brains are hardwired to do whatever it takes to keep us alive. While amazing in theory, remember that our genetic makeup goes all the way back to caveman days. Back then it was all about staying alive, which meant avoiding anything scary...which was pretty much everything in those days.

The "fight or flight" concept came from our very early ancestors...and back then the answer was mostly flight. Scientists have even started to research how this evolution created our current society's massive rise in anxiety. Long story short, really ask yourself if your fear is coming from a true survival standpoint or if it's just the caveman brain freaking you out. Always go back to the question: "Is this a legit thing I should be fearful of and avoid? Or does this fear take me away from who I really want to become?"

The big difference in reinvention and becoming who you really are is looking at the motivation for what you're doing. Do you REALLY want to hang out with the fancy neighbors and talk about the stock market? Or do you feel most comfortable with the messy moms having margaritas on a Tuesday?

Why is it so important for you to dress this way, be associated with these people, choose that career? Are you doing this for yourself or are you trying to prove a point to others? Really digging into your motivations and desired outcomes can help you break down whether or not something is helping you to become your most authentic self.

Exercise Time:
Create the Dream Life

The best way to practice this exercise is to sit down and think about where you see your ideal self in five years. Don't dwell on what you can or can't afford right now. Dream BIG on this one. When I do this exercise, I treat it as a meditation.

Here are some tips:

- Sit comfortably in a quiet place and close your eyes.

- Start visualizing your day as if you're just waking up.

- What do you see around you? Are you waking up in a giant loft downtown in a super king sized bed? Are you next to a partner in a farmhouse surrounded by dogs and kids? Take a moment to breathe in this imaginary life.

- Step-by-step work your way through your ideal day. Be sure to look around at what you see and how it makes you feel.

Once the visualization is done, slowly take a deep breath, open your eyes, and grab a journal. Write down everything you saw, did, and felt.

Then, ask yourself these big main questions:

• If money, time, and reality weren't a factor, what would you be doing?

• Who would you be with?

• Now work it back in your mind to today: "If this is where I want my life to go and who I want to be, how should I start living?" For example, if you see yourself backpacking in the mountains with your husband and kids, do you really NEED to schmooze with the people at the yacht club just because society tells you to? If you're traveling the world and crazy happy in this dream life, do you really NEED to buy a bigger house or lease a more expensive car? If you own your own business in this vision, who can you begin to surround yourself with?

Asking yourself what you ACTUALLY want (and don't want) out of life can help you to narrow down HOW you're setting yourself up now to become that person.

"Life is not tried, it's just merely survived if you're standing outside the fire."

~ Garth Brooks

Chapter Two:
First Big Holy Crap!

As kids we often learn that change is bad. So, what happens when the first big change hits? It could be your parents divorce, when you suddenly had two homes to bounce between. Perhaps it was a big move that changed everything and everyone you knew. Maybe it was when you suddenly graduated from high school and you're either thrown into the "real world" or you're off to college, away from everything you've ever known. Scary stuff!

Living my best life in high school, starring in all the school musicals, voted homecoming queen, and head-over-heels for my football-playing boyfriend, I wasn't worried about dominating the theater world in college and beyond. After being accepted into the musical theater program at Roosevelt University in downtown Chicago, I was pumped to live in a big city, away from home. I couldn't wait to visit my hometown as a full-on celebrity. But as soon as move-in day came and we arrived in Chicago, everything suddenly felt all wrong. I started to panic, begging my parents not to leave me there. I felt it in my gut that it was a bad move. I just KNEW if they left something awful would happen. Having already shelled out the thousands and thousands of dollars for college tuition, this of course was not an option.

Sadly, my worst nightmares came true. I hated the school and the weird theater kids. The college consisted of only one building which housed all of our classes AND our dorms, with no extracurricular activities. I felt trapped. The program that I had enrolled in focused on "Method Acting" which is a technique where you get into the character's mind to fully inhabit the role; drawing on your own pain to pull out emotions. In my opinion, this can be dangerous for those who aren't ready for it (aka 18-year-olds).

I went from being the bubbly class clown and Saturday Night Live addict in high school to a depressed mess who trudged up 11 flights of stairs to my dorm room just to avoid talking to people. Throw in a bad roommate and my first big love breaking up with me, and I was done. After popping a bunch of diet pills as a cry for help, I ended up moving home at the end of the first semester. Every fear of change had proven to be true; the world was a scary place and I should just play it safe and never leave my bubble again. This college experience justified it all! Or so I thought.

To say I felt like a weak failure was an understatement. My first big chance to get out of my hometown and I couldn't handle it. Coming home with my tail tucked between my legs was a humbling experience and it took me a while to recover. I don't think kids are prepared enough for the downswings and changes in life, and growing up in an era that didn't address mental health, I had no clue (until years later) that some of my high school friends were going through the same exact thing at the same exact time!

Can you imagine the relief we would've felt to know that we weren't alone or crazy? That we had an entire support system of people who could relate? A therapist suggested anti-depressants which I opted against. While I am not against medication for those who need it and struggle daily with mental health, I knew that what I was feeling was not my norm and that it was only temporary.

Instead, I went into "proactive mode" and created a plan of action for myself. I kept a calendar to track my good days, bad days, and unbearable days until there were no more unbearable days left. I made myself go for a walk every single day – even if I didn't feel like it (which was most days). I started journaling and mapping out what I would do next.

Give it Another Go!

When we are children we don't know how we'll deal with change. We never expect it to be quite as shocking or as scary as it can be. And if your first experience is anything like mine, it can set you up for an even BIGGER fear of change.

Years later, when I moved to Nashville, I freaked out on the drive there. "What if it was like my college experience?" I never even considered the alternative: what if it wasn't? The anxiety of going back out into the real world felt crippling to me. I remember saying to my dad, "But what if it doesn't work out again, and I hate it there?" My dad just replied with, "Then you leave."

It was that simple. It was in that moment I realized that nothing is forever, and sometimes that's ok. Heck, sometimes that's great! I was so convinced that I had something to "prove" by moving somewhere, that I had also tricked myself into believing that I could never change my mind if I didn't like it because...gasp...what would people think?!? But my dad was right! If I didn't like it, I could always leave. This also applies to careers, relationships, homes, etc. If you don't like it, you can leave.

Since I'd learned to equip myself with what to do during a big change, I was ready. Sure, I was nervous and skeptical of trying to leave my comfort zone again…but this time it turned out to be one of the greatest experiences of my life! I fell in love with Nashville. I felt fierce and strong going out on my own, and, for the first time in my life, I realized that sometimes facing a fear and embracing change is worth every anxiety-ridden moment.

No one can ever be fully prepared for life's biggest changes. Most pivots come because everything has shifted on its own and it's up to us to let go of the ledge and move forward, or keep a tight grip on the past that no longer serves us. It's ok if we get it wrong.

And we will. But don't be afraid to reach out and ask for help as you navigate these new waters. When it comes down to it, none of us really know what we're doing. But I do know that none of us are doing it alone.

Exercise Time:
Reflection and Remembering

- Write down some big changes from your past.

- For each big change, write down a list of things you did to navigate through; include things you did that didn't help.

- Now, write down some of the lessons you took away from that experience.

- Use the list to:

1. Begin creating a plan of action and steps to take when life shifts occur (you already have proof of what worked before).

2. Use this list to remind yourself that you are a complete badass who has survived change in the past, came out stronger, and learned a bunch from it!

"The secret of change is to focus all of your energy not on fighting the old but on building the new."

~ Socrates

Chapter Three:
The Big Ol' Rug Pull

Here's the problem with being a planner who doesn't like change: sometimes we go through with something we know isn't right simply because it was mapped out in our minds. We convince ourselves that whatever happens, we can force things to be ok.

My ex-husband and I had the ultimate meet-cute story, filled with butterflies and romance. In fact, after we first met I called my mom to say, "I've met the one!" It's the kind of story I'd always dreamed of. So, when a few weeks into the fairy tale, it wasn't living up to the story and red flags started popping up, I wouldn't let myself see them. He was the one! I'd already told everyone! I had reached the ripe-old spinster age of twenty-nine and had been single for just the right amount of time to become desperate. I believed this was my one and only shot at a "normal" life.

Two months into our relationship, I could no longer deny the red flags and we broke up. He went crazy trying to win me back, going so far as to hang a banner outside of his apartment that said, "I LOVE MONICA ORTEGA". He even showed me his savings for an engagement ring. Against my better judgement, I took him back. He was "Mr. Perfect" for three whole months until he got down on one knee. I finally felt like I was back on track, hitting all the milestones on this so-called ideal life timeline.

Of course, I knew things weren't right with every step of miserable wedding planning. What was supposed to be fun, turned into me begging him for things I wanted (a dynamic that should NEVER be happening in a relationship, by the way), including a honeymoon and to pay for a DJ rather than do it myself. Outrageous, I know! But when I asked my family and friends what they thought of him, I heard the same thing over and over again: "Wedding planning is stressful!" and "You're looking for a fairy tale and have unrealistic expectations" and "He's so charming, you'll never find better."

Here's a little tip for you – don't let anyone ever tell you you can't do any better or that your desires are unrealistic. Our loved ones can only support us with the information they have but no one knows your gut like you do! But we were so far in, I thought there was no going back. We'd already agreed on a life together; I was wearing the ring. And love conquers all, right?

If you find yourself in a situation of KNOWING something isn't right and no one has told you this yet…just know that it's perfectly ok to LEAVE.

Surprisingly, the marriage didn't save our relationship! Who woulda thunk it? It was a narcissistic cycle of being told I expected too much, being rejected constantly, feeling depressed, and then being made to feel like it was all my fault.

We'd had all of the important "talks" before getting married: Do you want kids? What are your goals? Do you like the outdoors? Suddenly, once the vows were said and done, so were his thoughts on everything he said he wanted. He no longer wanted kids, or a house, or a dog, or apparently a wife. I felt trapped. Needless to say, it wasn't my favorite time in life.

After nearly four years into an emotionally abusive marriage, I was checked out. The only silver lining for me was – when I realized he wouldn't travel or adventure with me – I started my online travel show, *Monica Goes*. Heading out on adventures kept me sane and happy through the depression and hopelessness that filled my home life.

One day, my ex offered to go hiking with me. He even helped me film, which I found bizarre since that was never an option! We had an incredible day. Just as I felt a glimmer of hope...the next morning, everything changed.

I woke up to him telling me he had a confession to make. He explained that a girl he'd gone on a couple of dates with before we met, was threatening my life because she had just found out he was married. Um... what?

He explained she was angry when he didn't continue to date her and she blew up when she found out he was engaged. So "for my protection" he had been hanging out with her to "keep her calm." Um... what?

At this point, I had to laugh at the absurdity of it all. I said I wished he would have told me, so I could be aware if she ever came around. I asked what he meant by "hanging out" to which he replied, "We watch movies and stuff." Um...WHAT?!?

I couldn't believe it. He'd been going to this person's house for four years to "watch movies" and nothing else had ever happened? Finally, he said, "I mean, sometimes we cuddle." Yeah...no!

At this point, in a state of shock, in my pajamas, I got up and mindlessly started to put random belongings into a suitcase and headed to a friend's apartment. I later found out that, as suspected, he did much more than "cuddle" and honestly this girl had had every right to be angry after finding out he was married!

Later that night, still in shock, I headed to the restaurant where I worked, laughing with coworkers about my situation. About 30 minutes before closing, I went out to the patio and I collapsed. Out of nowhere, I was struggling to breathe. It was my first full on panic attack.

The next few days were a blur of looking at apartments, talking to lawyers, and researching everything I could about divorce. This, combined with him breaking down begging for me to take him back, and also the odd sensation of relief and joy I felt that I could finally leave! I was free! This wasn't a pivot.

This was a full-on world flip.

An *"entire floor being pulled out from underneath me"* type of change. But the biggest emotion I felt during this time was *hope*.

Why do I share all of this? Well, there will be times in your life where you'll also have to deal with HUGE, GIANT, UNPLANNED pivots. The kind that you just KNOW you will not be coming out the same from.

Those big start-over moments where you are left standing in the dust that was once your life, asking yourself, "What now?"

At which point you may experience…

The Rollercoaster of Emotions Will Come at Random Times

There are a range of emotions that will come and go in giant waves when this kind of rug-pull occurs. They will happen when you're fully expecting them to, surrounded by friends, ready to break down. And then they'll also pop up five years down the road when you're having the best day, until suddenly you can't get a jar of sauce open and you're left in a pool of tears wondering how you could ever end up so alone. Get ready! But it's not all bad! In fact, some of it can be pretty darn awesome. It's all about shifting your mindset.

One of the biggest things I've heard from people who've been through a divorce or lost a loved one in another way, is that it's when everyone around you goes back to their regular lives and stops checking in with you that it can hit the hardest.

When something traumatic happens, friends and family rush in to help. I had SO many people calling and texting and messaging me to check in during those first couple of months. But the weird thing is that, in those first couple of months, I felt great! I was in go-mode, looking forward to the next chapter of my life. Things hadn't really sunk in yet.

It wasn't until about a year later, when everyone was back to their "real" lives and I'd moved into a great place, things were finalized, and life seemed grand – that's when the emotions and panic attacks hit me out of nowhere. It felt irrational! I'd become furious with myself (which doesn't help anything, by the way). "Why can't you just be over it? Why are you crying now?" But that's the thing about trauma…healing isn't a linear process. Something random would pop up out of nowhere and I'd be triggered all over again.

I had started dating someone new and one night I found myself swallowing popcorn kernels whole because I didn't want him to be "put off" by my chewing too loudly (something my ex had used as a reason not to hang out with me). Once I explained to this guy why I had been silent most of the night, he showed up to our next date with a big bag of popcorn and said, "I expect to hear you chewing every bite".

Little moments like that made me realize my scars may be a little deeper than I'd thought. And little moments like chewing popcorn in front of a guy I'd just met, slowly helped me to heal.

Your Trauma Might Make Others Uncomfortable and That's Their Problem – Not Yours

I'm an open book type of person (I mean, I am writing a book after all!). I'm also a huge believer that we go through things to share our stories and connect with others. But I can also respect the fact that not everyone feels the same way. Older generations sometimes have a harder time opening up. Our parents and grandparents grew up learning to not "air your dirty laundry" for everyone. But I believe so much shame and emotional distress comes from believing we are the ONLY ones who've ever dealt with this, and if we don't have it all figured out then there must be something wrong with us.

To this day, my friends and family don't mention my ex or the big "D" word. If I make a joke about him they quickly change the subject. This was hard at first because it was still a big part of my life and something that had happened to me. To ignore the five years I was with him also disregarded all of the lessons I took with me afterward, not to mention the progress I'd made as a human through all of this.

Over the years, it bothered me less and less because 1. I stopped talking about it as much as I was moving on, 2. I learned which friends and family members I could have those heart-to-heart chats with, and 3. the older I get, the more I realize we're all just doing the best we can with what we know. I appreciate the people who were just trying to protect my heart and keep me from feeling uncomfortable.

In Sheryl Sandberg's book *Option B*, she talks about unexpectedly losing her husband. She writes, "We all live some sort of Option B...The elephant is always there. By ignoring it, those who are grieving isolate themselves and those who could offer comfort create distance instead."

Never let anyone make you feel ashamed of what you've gone through, good or bad, your fault or not. But also understand that not everyone will feel as comfortable talking about your pivots and changes.

Especially if they're sad, nervous, or jealous about the changes you've made in your life. Find a tribe that cheers you on through life's pivots and cling to them! And as Sandberg writes in her book,

"Option A is not available, so let's just kick the shit out of Option B!"

It's Ok to Not Be Ok

This just goes for life in general and I will say it many times. It's ok to not be ok. You don't need to justify it or explain it to anyone. It's ok to not be ok. I was so focused on moving on and using my trauma to inspire others that I didn't actually deal with it right away.

When it would hit, I had to bypass the urge to be angry at myself for not being ok and give myself a break. Let yourself feel your emotions, ride them out, and remember: it's ok to not be ok.

Exercise Time:
Ready for the Rollercoaster

I made a plan for breakups that applies pretty well to traumatic events in general. We all have different emotions that hit on different days so I like to have options for whatever I'm feeling that day. After a breakup, I had a variety of things I could try to help me get through the ensuing days:

- Spend the day watching sappy movies and hysterically crying.

- Get dressed up and have a full on solo dance party.

- Call up my girlfriends for a night out and flirty rebound.

- Call up my girlfriends for a night full of ice cream and rom-coms.

- Treat myself to a spa day - hello, self-care mode!

- Journal, meditate, pray, and all the woo-woo goodness to shift my mindset.

- Go on an angry run to burn it off.

- And so on…

The same solution won't work every day or every time but keeping a list of options to ride out my emotions helped me to feel proactive and in some sort of control.

So, when the rollercoaster of emotions starts to kick in, go through your list, pick one (or five!) things and start to test out what gets you through it.

Give yourself the space to grieve the loss of what was and remember: it's ok to not be ok.

It's Ok to Be Happy

This was always a weird one to have to remind myself, especially when society tells you that you **should** feel a certain way. First off, screw the word **should**. In fact, **should** and **shouldn't** can go piss off! In my opinion, these are two of the worst words in the English language.

No one **should** do anything! Who says? "I **should** get married" got me into this whole mess in the first place, so "I **shouldn't** be happy alone" can also go screw itself. In the words of Sex in the City's Carrie Bradshaw, "Why are we should'ing all over ourselves?"

But that's easier said than done. Especially when someone else is hurting. It was always awkward to see my ex breaking down in tears and begging my forgiveness, while on the inside I was thinking, "Cool bro, you can have it. I've got a date with a hottie later anyway." I know that sounds callous and – trust me – there was plenty of sadness too, but inside I was psyched!

It's ok to be hopeful about the changes you want to make. It's ok to be pumped that you get a do-over. It's ok to be happy. And if people want to judge your happiness, well they can join **should** and **shouldn't** in the screw off pile.

When a huge life-altering change happens, the biggest thing I can say is **be easy on yourself**. Just because others have gone through that before doesn't mean YOU have. It's all new and each day is going to come with its own challenges and victories.

Don't compare how you're handling this shock and trauma with anyone else. Do what's best for you and take it all one day at a time. It's ok to not be ok.

"This is a good sign, having a broken heart. It means we have tried for something."

~ Elizabeth Gilbert

Chapter Four:
The Joys of Mental Illness

Mental illness is such an odd term. Even writing it, I can feel the tension. Some of you may be thinking, "I'm not crazy, I can just skip this chapter!" But hear me out. Saying "I have an illness" when talking about a cold isn't weird, right?

So, why does "mental illness" get such a bad rap?

And just like any other type of illness, some of us may have a cold or a flu-type illness where it just sort of hits us out of nowhere a couple of times a year; others have a chronic illness like diabetes or Lyme disease where it just becomes a part of life. Remember, we can blame it all on the cavemen.

I'm going to preface this chapter by saying that I am not a mental health expert. I can only offer advice based on what I've learned from my own experiences. If you are struggling with depression, anxiety, and/or suicidal thoughts please get professional help. Seek out a licensed therapist.

I believe we can ALL benefit from therapy anyway; I highly recommend it!

To reiterate:

1. I'm not an expert.

2. Having a mental illness doesn't mean you're crazy.

3. My knowledge and experiences have been more sporadic rather than chronic.

4. Therapy is awesome!

As I've mentioned, my first bout of "Whoa, I guess I'm not ok all the time" came during college when I became extremely depressed and had no idea what to do about it. I felt as if I was floating above myself, watching this shell of a person slug through the day-to-day. I wanted to scream at her, "Wake up and stop being so lame!" But I was too numb to care. Also, negative self talk and beating yourself up for not being ok doesn't really help the situation either!

The next level of mental illness hit me like a freight train. The night I left my husband, working as a server at the Cheesecake Factory where I experienced my first panic attack out on the patio. Both of these experiences took me by surprise and made me feel out of control, which is something I hate! But, as I mentioned, I am a big-time planner and I feel more stable knowing I have a "tool kit" to dig into when these mood shifts occur.

One of the biggest side effects of a sudden change in our lives can be an onslaught of emotions we never saw coming, leading to depression and/or anxiety. If you're like me and had never experienced this before, it can be super scary! Even if you've never experienced these emotions before, my advice is to treat it like a natural disaster or an animal attack...even if it never happens, it's better to be prepared and know what to do – just in case!

First off, know that you're not crazy! Our brains are freaking weird! We use so little of them and scientists are still trying to understand them. Don't get all weirded out if you find yourself in a sudden spiral you never saw coming. Remember, be easy on yourself and it's ok to not be ok.

Next, know that you're not weak! In the same way I have a hard time forgiving myself, I also have a hard time not beating myself up when I'm not ok. We all want to think we can just mentally pull ourselves out when we start spiraling. One of the worst things you can do at the beginning of a mental spiral is to get angry at yourself for it.

Imagine thinking, "He didn't call me so I bet he doesn't like me." And then the spiral starts…"Wow, I can't believe it, I thought I was awesome!" "What did I do so wrong to make him not like me?" "This always happens to me." "I suck; everyone leaves me because I'm so awful and I'll be alone forever." Then, adding onto it and getting mad. "Wow, I really am pathetic!" "Listen to me! I sound stupid feeling sorry for myself; why can't I just be happy?" "I'm so pathetic I can't even be happy - no wonder everyone hates me."

Beating yourself up for not being able to "just be happy" only adds more self-loathing to an already spiraling brain. That's like adding gasoline to a fire and getting mad when the flames don't burn out.

How to Stop the Spiral

"A thought is harmless unless we believe it. It's not our thoughts, but the attachment to our thoughts, that causes suffering. Attaching to a thought means believing that it's true, without inquiring. A belief is a thought that we've been attaching to, often for years." ~ Byron Katie, *Loving What Is: Four Questions That Can Change Your Life*

The key with a spiraling brain is to get ahead of it and stop the spiral. Now that I know my brain does this, I make it a mission to try to find the ACTUAL truth before letting myself come up with lies. Sometimes it takes writing it out and asking myself, is this REALLY true?

"He didn't call me so I bet he doesn't like me" simply becomes "He didn't call me." That's the ONLY truth. His reason for not calling could be a million different things.

It's all about switching your mindset. Rather than thinking "He doesn't like me", switch it to "I know I'm awesome and, if he doesn't call, that's his loss". You can do this with every sentence your brain creates to find out if it's really true. Catch yourself in the lie.

Sometimes, when we're in a spiral, it's REALLY hard to pull the truth out. Like in *Who Wants to Be a Millionaire*, when you don't know the answer, it's time to 'phone a friend.' My best friend knows I can spiral, so sometimes I'll call her and say, "Ok, I'm spiraling and I need to know if this is true and justified." She'll disprove it in about three seconds, helping to stop the spiral before it happens. Using actual facts helps.

Before you go down a spiral of negative thinking, consider if something is real and true, or if it's just a story you're telling yourself. For example, you might say:

"I'm a crappy friend."

To which your friend might say, "Oh really? Because last week you bought Jennifer flowers just because. And you threw a surprise party for Taylor! And you answer the phone anytime I need you."

"Oh ok," you say, "I guess you're right." Boom, spiral prevented!

If you don't have a friend who is available to talk, just consider what you'd say if the tables were turned. Try to remove yourself from the situation and be your own best friend. Focus on the facts. Now tell those negative thoughts to piss off because no one talks to my bestie that way!

Build a Spiral Tool Kit

I find the true balance of happiness, for me, comes in doing my best to create the life that I desire and to avoid downfalls as much as possible. I do this by building up a tool kit and creating a plan for all the good AND all the bad that may come my way. The goal is being able to let it go and ride the waves as they come. In the same way that we can manifest the most incredible things in our lives, we can also manifest some pretty dark stuff if we're not careful. One of the most heartbreaking things I hear is when people say, "I had a breakdown but I'm fine now; I'm on the other side of it and it won't happen again." I once sat down with a friend who confessed that a month earlier he had nearly committed suicide; To the point of having the letter all written out and everything. But he quickly brushed it off and said, "I'm fine now though so don't worry. It was just a rough time and I know that won't happen again."

Here's the thing: once you've felt depressed or had even one anxiety attack, there's a GOOD chance it will happen again in your lifetime. Maybe not as severely and maybe not for another 15 years, but we never know when something traumatic may happen – and before we know it, we could be spiraling hardcore.

So, instead of trying to just muscle it out and convince ourselves that we are strong enough to handle anything, why not just accept the fact that bad stuff is going to happen in our lives? And that's normal! Knowing how to deal with it can help to take the fear out of what to do if/when it happens – it may even save your life.

Think of it this way: Anxiety is our emotions wrapped up in fear; often the fear of what MIGHT happen. So you spend all this time terrified something bad is going to happen and then – BOOM! – it does. Because, as we all know, life certainly isn't perfect or pretty all the time. So something bad happens and you continue to spiral into depression because the thing you were so afraid of happening did… Now, you build up MORE fear of it happening again and the cycle continues. Phew!

Being proactive about your mental health can come in handy when things start going downhill. In the same way I have my relationship-ending tool kit, I also put one together for depression and anxiety. Here are a few examples that work for me:

Depression

When the cold, numbness of depression starts kicking in, here are some strategies I use to pull myself out before it gets too dark and dreary:

• **Call someone:** friend, family, or a therapist – force yourself against all of your inner feelings to talk to a human. The irony of depression is that that's usually the LAST thing you want to do. But it's often the most important and beneficial. I've gone down the whole, "No one wants to be dragged down by my sadness" line of thinking but if they love you, they'll be there. And if it is becoming a chronic thing that your friends and family are having a hard time helping you with, that's where a good old-fashioned therapist comes in! It's their job to listen and help you during these times.

• **Let yourself be sad but give yourself a time limit.** Knowing you get one full day to lay in bed and feel all the feels, will help you to feel less guilty and avoid beating yourself up. It also forces you to have to change it up the next day. Even if it's just, "Ok, I get 30 minutes to scream and cry and then I'm going to go run it out!"

• **Be careful what you're taking in** - books, TV, food, all of it. We're more mentally affected by the things we surround ourselves with and what we put into our bodies than we realize. There have been studies done on how watching violent video games or constantly taking in depressing stories can actually begin to rewire our brains. Instead, fuel yourself with things that make you feel better. Watch funny shows, read inspiring books, eat nutritious foods. Trust me, I know when I'm depressed, ice cream and wine sound like the perfect solution...but that's not always the best move.

- **Get active!** Working out naturally releases endorphins which will help to boost your mood. Even if you don't feel like it when you start, your brain will thank you afterward. Focusing on breathing and getting through the workout will help to take your mind off of the spiral. So get out and simply go for a walk if that's all you can manage for now.

- **Get some D!** Vitamin D that is. Vitamin D is another natural mood booster, so go for a walk or just lay in the sun for a bit. I've even just sat inside near a window with my eyes closed to take in those sweet, sweet, rays. It will help you feel much better than if you were to crawl back under the covers, I promise.

- **Say yes to the invites!** Every instinct when you're down is to hide away and think, "No one wants to be around me like this." But getting out will naturally boost your mood and help you move past the funk. Bonus points if those invites are for a fun activity. Doing something adventurous can require so much focus that it pushes you to be present and less stuck inside your dark brain.

- **Spend time with kids or animals.** It's hard to feel the worst when you're surrounded by something or someone who always feels their best. Kids and animals have a way of comforting us just with their presence and carefree way of living. They can shift our perspectives to what's really important – like cuddles and playing!

• **Put on real clothes.** While your coffee-stained sweats are comfy, getting dressed in something that makes you feel good will help boost your confidence. For an added bonus, do your hair and makeup!

• **Dance it out.** This is always my go-to! Blast the music and go for it!

Anxiety

Right around the time that I was feeling good about my 'depression tool kit' that I had been building since college, I had my first panic attack at work. I was like, "What the what?!? I'm hyper and I can't breathe; I wanna run a marathon and also cry. I don't get it!"

Anxiety is a totally different beast. When depression hits, you can barely move, but when anxiety kicks in you can't stop. Yet, many of the solutions are the same. Here are some things that have worked for me in the past:

• **Work it out** - In addition to releasing all those good endorphins, an anxiety workout may be a bit more hardcore. Power run, kickboxing, swimming…anything fast-paced that can tire out your muscles and your brain are all good! This can also be a positive side effect of anxiety if you learn how to utilize it. "Hey Sheila, what kind of diet are you doing? You look amazing!" "Thanks, it's all my anxiety runs!"

• **Meditation** - We'll get a bit more into this later, but forcing yourself to stop and attempting to clear the mind can do wonders. This can be SUPER hard when your brain is racing, so if you can't seem to settle into silence, I recommend a guided meditation to try to fight off all of the noise.

• **Prayer** - If you are a person of faith like me, remember to lean into that. Trusting God can help stop your anxious fears.

"Cast all of your anxiety on Him because he cares for you." 1 Peter 5:7

• **Cook** - Putting your brain into a task can help you to stay focused and stop your thoughts from wandering. Of course, this can be applied to any task, like scrapbooking, knitting, playing video games, etc.

- **Adventure** - In the same way that cooking helps you to focus on a task, going on an adventure that forces you to concentrate and stay present can be a great way to put your brain to use in a more positive way. It's hard to overthink any problems when you're rock climbing and looking for the next foothold, or while rafting down a raging river listening to your guide's calls.

- **Read** - Reading slows your heart rate and helps you focus on something other than your own thoughts. As with depression, you'll want to read positive things to boost your mood. Out with the bad, in with the good!

- **Switch to decaf** - If I know my anxiety has been kicking in I'll switch to caffeine-free drinks and limit my alcohol consumption. These changes can also help you sleep better, which can be tricky with anxiety. Can't give up the caffeine? Try mixing in half decaf with your regular cup of Joe, limit yourself to one cup, and/or cut yourself off earlier in the day.

- **Stream of conscious writing** - Sometimes it's just a matter of letting yourself say (or write) all of the things that are in your head. Without any judgement or thought, give yourself permission, let yourself go, and write whatever comes to mind. It could be complete gibberish or something thought-provoking – it doesn't matter. Bonus: If you're finding a lot of negative talk pop up in your writing, go back to disproving yourself and rewrite those sentences to capture what's **actually** true.

• **Use your senses.** Hold your hand up and look around. Recognize something you see, something you can touch, something you smell, something you taste, and something you hear. As you go through each one, touch your thumb to each finger or put each finger down one at a time. Doing this can help pull a spiraling brain back to the present by initiating all five senses.

• **Dance it out** - Always keep dancing!

Exercise Time:
Create Your Mental Tool Kit

• Sit down with a pen and paper and start to write down anything you've done in the past to deal with anxiety or depression. Make note of things that really helped you get through it. Begin creating your own tool kit to stay proactive when your brain kicks into a mental downswing.

• Write a letter to yourself reminding yourself of how awesome you are! This sounds super cheesy but trust me, when the going gets tough, it can be super helpful to read this back. Bonus: In your letter remind yourself of how you've been through things like this before and you know that you're strong enough to handle this again. It can be a lifeline when your brain is telling you that you can't make it through this.

• Keep a gratitude journal. I go back and forth on this one. Sometimes it's super helpful to put things into perspective. I have a home, I have food, I have a job, etc. It's awesome to be grateful for what you have and to remind yourself of how blessed you are. But be careful to make sure you're not using this as a way to beat yourself up.

For example, some people will think, "Well, I **should** be happy, I have a home and some people don't" or "Why do I feel like crap? I have no business feeling like crap, I have a job and others don't!" If writing out your blessings pulls you out of a mental spiral by putting things in perspective, awesome! If it's pulling you further down, trash it and try something else! It's ok to realize what works for you and what doesn't and try something new. It's ok to not be ok.

"Promise me you'll always remember — You're braver than you believe, and stronger than you seem, and smarter than you think."

~ Christopher Robin from "Winnie the Pooh"

Chapter Five:
Let The Good Vibes Flow & Let The Crap People Go

Forgiveness and Moving On

I hate the term "Forgive and Forget." Not because of the forgiveness part but, rather, it's the forgetting I have an issue with. And this isn't a case of "Screw them, I never forget anything" so you can hold onto a grudge. But I believe that some of life's greatest gifts are the hardships that we go through. Sounds crazy, right? But it's true! We grow so much during times of adversity and the most valuable lessons often come from our biggest heartaches.

So, yes, forgive, forgive, forgive – but never forget.

Forgiveness 101

Someone hurting you is never fun but, like the quote says:

"Not forgiving someone is like drinking poison and expecting the other person to die." ~Unknown

When we hold onto grudges, we are actually punishing ourselves more than anyone, because chances are, the other person has already moved on and they're probably not thinking about you as much as you wish they were. When we choose not to forgive someone, we're also holding tightly to our pain which stops us from letting ourselves heal and grow; essentially, we're stuck. Forgiving people who hurt you is never easy. Here are some things that have helped me:

See the Broken Kid Inside

One of the easiest ways for me to forgive my ex was to see him as a broken little boy and to try to understand what made him into the person he became. At his core, he was a good person, doing the best he could with who he was. Of course, that does not excuse his actions (doing that would be like seeing SO much good in him that I decided to stay married in the hopes that he could change into his potential).

On that note, **never** fall in love with someone's potential. Just because you see who they **might** possibly, one day, become doesn't mean they actually want that or that they will ever turn into that person. You're only wasting your own awesomeness on someone who's not ready for it.

Seeing the broken child inside allows you to understand that their intention was never to destroy your life, only to save theirs. I once asked my ex why he married me. He said, "I thought you could save me." Don't stay with someone because you think they can "fix" you or that you can "fix" them. It's a recipe for disaster.

It's also important to take a good hard look at yourself and try to uncover your own broken child. When I did that, I was able to step back and realize that I had gotten married because the kid in me believed that love could conquer all, and that there's good in everyone. I had also convinced myself that I couldn't have a career and a relationship and that I was falling behind on some sort of imaginary timeline. Doing this internal digging into the motivations behind my actions helped me to forgive myself for not initially listening to my gut and for continuing down a rough path. Once you see that they (and you) did the best they could, forgive.

Remember the Good

This is a **really** tricky one for a few reasons. I had a hard time finding the balance between remembering the good and feeling like I was letting my ex off easily, or spiraling into blaming myself for looking back fondly and getting myself there in the first place. But it's important to remember that things weren't always bad and this person didn't always hurt you. Again, people do the best they can with what they know.

As I mentioned, trauma is a rollercoaster of emotions. For the first year, I bounced between anxious excitement and hope at the blank page I suddenly had to write for my future, and anger and sadness. I was angry and sad at my ex for hurting me, but also at myself for marrying him at all, staying with him, missing him – you name it! I felt a heavy burden of guilt for going through with the wedding.

It didn't help that, out of anger, I kept telling people about all of the red flags that I saw when we were engaged and how it all ended and they would say, "Wow! Why would you marry that guy?"

It took me a long time before I was ready to accept that I wasn't stupid and that I didn't marry some horrible monster. There were good things, too. Finally, when I was ready, I let myself sift through the happy photos and memories, grieve the loss, and I learned to eventually forgive myself.

One of the easiest ways for me to forgive my ex was to remind myself that he didn't HAVE to come clean. At the end of the day, he did the right thing even though he knew he'd risk losing me.

He set me free with his honesty and that took a LOT of bravery on his part. I will always be grateful to him for that.

Forgive Yourself While You're at It

I have a much harder time letting myself off the hook than I do others. I hold myself to very high standards, so when other people hurt me I tend to believe that I did it to myself. I guess I deserved it, right? Whoa whoa whoa there negative nelly! That kind of thinking is incredibly self-destructive and doesn't help you become the awesome human you're meant to be.

Telling yourself you deserve the things that happened in your past is wiring your brain to believe that you don't deserve anything good in the future. Not very hopeful or exciting, eh?

Remember, the same way others are doing the best they can with what they know and who they are, is the same way YOU did the best you could with what you knew and who you were. Thank that person who did their best back then and be super stoked that you're not that human anymore.

How would you have learned all the great stuff and grown without making those choices? In the end, there's no wrong choice because it's already done. Let it go and move on.

Not Everyone Will be Here For the Pivot

A big part of changing and pivoting is that it also changes those around you. One of the hardest lessons for me to accept growing up was that people come into your life for different seasons. While this can be tough to accept, I promise it gets easier as you get older. Not everyone is meant to be a forever friend…and that's ok.

It's the same way that not everyone you date is meant to be the person you'll marry. Can you imagine trying to force a marriage out of that weird date you went on with the guy who showed up two hours late, barely said two words, and chewed with his mouth open?? Oof!

As humans, we all want to be liked and I think women, especially, feel the need to "fix" relationships way past their expiration date. Sometimes it serves both people better to simply let go and move on.

But ending relationships with friends and family members can be just as painful (if not worse) than romantic relationships because we truly believed that they would be there forever.

Pain Makes Some People Uncomfortable

So often after losing a loved one through divorce or death, friends drift away. Maybe they don't know how to handle your sadness or they just don't know what to say. Maybe it reminds them too much of their own losses or they feel like they can no longer relate. I had people tell me they were uncomfortable sharing their good news of marriages and kids with me because they thought it would make me sad.

The funny thing is, I attended a friend's wedding only a month after I left my ex and it had the opposite effect. It left me so hopeful and stoked to see what REAL love looked like and know that I now had the chance to go after it again.

Sometimes it's just a matter of having those awkward conversations. I was feeling so alone and left out when people didn't share their lives with me but I had no idea they were just trying not to hurt me. Once I explained that I wanted and sometimes NEEDED to be reminded of all of the good and exciting things life had to offer, those conversations opened back up and friendships were healed.

Success Makes Some People Uncomfortable

In the same way some people can be uncomfortable around people's pain, others are uncomfortable around people's success. One of the hardest losses in my life was my best friend who was there through all of the painful bits but slowly drifted away and started to distance herself as I became more happy and successful.

People like things that are familiar, and sometimes that may be a dynamic of a relationship. Maybe your big sister is used to you being the family "screw up" and, now that things are taking off for you, she doesn't know how to act if she's not cleaning up your mess. Maybe you have a friend who likes being the shoulder you cry on because it makes her feel needed – but now that you're strong and powerful, she feels left out. Maybe you know someone who's unhappy with their own life choices and resents the fact that you don't have the same responsibilities as them.

No matter what the situation and dynamic may be, it's ok to let go of toxic relationships. I will say, first things first: I recommend talking to your loved one and letting them know that you're feeling a distance or animosity. Try to repair the relationship before bailing altogether. Sometimes it's a misunderstanding or they simply need to hear you say you'll always need them/love them/etc. But if you've expressed how you feel and they continue to resent your success and remain unsupportive, it's ok to begin to let them go.

Understanding that relationships change in seasons is part of growing up. I believe we meet people exactly when we're supposed to, and they can be an epic part of your life during that time. And it's also ok if you both grow and change and no longer find yourselves with the same things in common. The most important thing is to leave everything in love.

I was heartbroken when I eventually realized my friendship was one-sided. When I stepped back and she never reached out, I knew that it was ok to move on. I will always be here if she ever needs me and I will always love and appreciate our friendship for the years it lasted, but I will no longer waste my energy trying to mend a friendship that has out-grown itself.

Find Your Tribe

One of the biggest keys to success and creating a life you love is to surround yourself with people who light you up, love you unconditionally, and push you to be your best. Look for mentors and friends who work in careers you'd love to have and learn from them. Surround yourself with happy, optimistic people who won't let you stay in the dumps for long; people who remind you to have fun! Have a few people who call it like they see it and hold you accountable for being your best self. Once you find these friendships, cherish them and have a kickass life together!

Letting people go is one of the most painful and necessary things in our lives. You'd never want to continue dating someone who complains all the time, puts you down, is jealous of your success, and is just an all around doo-doo head. So don't be afraid to break up with friends and/or family members who do the same. Mentally thank them for everything they've brought into your life and then let them go in love.

So let's figure out what qualities you look for and cherish in your dream tribe. After my divorce, one of the things my therapist had me do was write down a list of non-negotiables, as well as a list of qualities I liked in others. She explained to me that a not-so-fun side effect of divorce is being afraid to trust yourself again.

"I made this crappy decision, how can I be assured I won't make it again?" First off, forgive yourself! Having this list really helped me to steer clear of what I knew I didn't want, and to know what I absolutely needed in a partner. It also helped me avoid my usual pitfall of seeing the potential in someone and using that to excuse the way they treated me. On a first date I could look at the non-negotiable list and say, "Nope, he doesn't want kids. I know we had a fun first date but there's no reason to go out again."

For friendships, I think it's also important to look at qualities you value in those you choose to surround yourself with. The non-negotiables may be less important because you don't have to marry them but they're still vital, as these are people you'll spend a lot of time with. Look at the friends you admire and the qualities they embody and create a list of things to look for in new relationships. Find values that align with your own.

Really want to up your game and surround yourself with high-vibe people? Make a point to look for people who are living the kind of life you want to live and see if there's a potential friendship there. Hang around people with more success, more money, better health, and happier outlooks.

If you're constantly hanging out with people who are just barely getting by and are unambitious in their own lives, it'll be tough to stay motivated and optimistic yourself. Make friends in high places and then thrive together.

Exercise Time:
Set Up Your Own Dream Team!

"Who and what we surround ourselves with is who and what we become. In the midst of good people, it is easy to be good. in the midst of bad people, it is easy to be bad." ~ Karen Marie Moning

Look around your circle at the people who mean the most to you. Make a list of why you love them. Do they motivate you? Are they good listeners? Do they call you out on your bullshit? Whatever it is, write it down. Then, write down qualities you want to surround yourself with; trustworthy, great sense of humor, loves the outdoors.

Making friends is kinda like dating. You have to hang out to see if you like each other and have future potential. Some work out, others don't.

Make it a point to seek out people who vibe high with you, and together you can create a kickass life.

Bonus: Call up the friends that you value and let them know why!

"I get by with a little help from my friends."

~ The Beatles

Chapter Six:
Get Back To You
The New and Improved You!

One of the hardest things about a shift in your life is knowing who you are without x, y, and z. When things change, for good or bad, you will change too. And that's scary. Think of an NFL player who gets seriously injured. For however many years they've defined themselves as a football player; it's all they've done since they were a kid, it's who they were in college, and what they did for work. Suddenly, in one split second, they can never play football again. The big question becomes, "If I'm not a football player, then who am I?" This is the same in any situation: "If I'm not a husband, who am I?" or "If I'm not the fun, single friend who dances on tables, who am I?"

Well, what better time to figure it out then now?! Remember, no one cares about you as much as you think they do. It sounds harsh, I know. But it can actually be quite liberating. We're all in our own heads freaking out about how everyone else is viewing us.

The truth is, they're stuck in their own heads freaking out about the same thing so there's no room for you up there! So it's ok to take the time to figure out who you were, who you are now, and who you want to be.

Remembering Who You Are

There's looking ahead at all of the exciting things you want to be and who you can become and then there's looking back and trying to remind yourself of who you were before. One of the hardest things for me after my divorce was regaining a sense of self.

I'd become this shell of a person, just trying to make someone else happy for so many years, I'd forgotten all about the badass awesome person I was when he initially met me!

One thing my therapist had me do was write down all of the things I used to do before I met my ex. Then, simply, start doing them! No matter how foreign or uncomfortable it felt now.

She also had me write down all of the things I wanted to do but felt like I couldn't in my marriage.

This was my list:

- Travel
- Sing in a band
- Sing in the shower
- Dance around
- Have a home everyone was welcome in
- Be an open book again
- Get a dog
- Live on my own again
- Try stand up comedy

Then, one by one, I started forcing myself to book the trip, call up the old band, sign up for an open mic, and get the damn dog! Slowly, as I put the actions into place, the old confidence I had began to trickle back in as well. With each action, I gained a little more strength in knowing I had control over my life.

Don't forget to put yourself out there and try some new things as well! Who knows what the current, badass version of you may like! And, remember, try everything TWICE!

Take Back the Memories

When I was in middle school I decided my lucky number was 1017. I started seeing the number everywhere. From football scores ending in 10-17 to radio stations scanning and stopping on 101.7. It became my thing. So, in high school, I decided I would get married on the 17th of October. It was my lucky day, after all. When I met my ex I told him on our second date that my plan was to get married October 17, and that's exactly what we did; Thursday and all.

As the first 17th of October approached after I had left him, I was feeling pretty sad and anxious. Then, I was angry – my special day was gone! But then I thought, screw it. It was MY day before him and I was going to make damn sure it would be my day after him too. I was taking my day back! To celebrate my special day, I headed out to Death Valley and went on my first solo camping trip. I brought along my guitar and the fancy bottle of wine that I never seemed to have a special enough occasion for. I ended up drinking, singing, and even streaking through the desert simply because I could! It was epic! To this day, every year I still get excited for the 17th of October. It's become my "me day!" I try to go on an adventure, have a spa day, or just do whatever my little heart desires. People have begun wishing me a happy lucky day every year.

Side note: If you don't have a "lucky day," I highly recommend choosing one for yourself! Holidays are so full of traditions and expectations, and birthdays end up being all about the parties and celebrations with family and friends. Everyone deserves one day during the year that's just for them, to do whatever they like. So pick a day of the year and make it your special "me day".

Listen to the songs they took from you, go to the places you loved previously. Don't be afraid to take back the memories for yourself again. I'm a big believer in not giving anyone the power to decide how you feel or what you like. Never let anything be off limits because of another person.

After a relationship ends, so many people think, "Oh man, I can't go there, I used to go there with so and so…" or "Change the station, this was my favorite song until it became my song with so and so."

Screw that! Go back to that kickass destination and blare that awesome song! Each time you do, you'll create a new memory that's just for you, and those old memories will start fading into the background. Take back your badass power!

Out With the Bad, in With the Good

A pivot is an incredible time to take stock of what's working for you and what's not working in your life. Look back on the people, things, and qualities of your "previous" life that you loved. Then find a way to recreate as much of that goodness moving forward as you can. Finally, look back at what didn't work and leave it in love. Businesses do this every quarter when they reassess their sales, strategies, and goals; it's time we start doing that in our own lives too.

Use this time to dream of what you never imagined yourself being or having, and figure out a plan to become that person now. Maybe before this you were super tight with your family and you don't want to lose that. Well, ok, schedule those things into your new and improved life. But maybe you drank too much and that was a problem, so consciously make a point to only drink when you're socializing with friends. Or maybe you've never meditated, but in this ideal version of yourself you're a meditator. Start looking into what it entails and set aside five minutes to make it a part of your daily routine.

When life pulls a 180 degree turn on you, rather than seeing how what you had is over and gone, start to look at all the possibilities of what you can develop now. Don't be afraid to look back and piece together how you step forward from here. Create that life you love!

Exercise Time:
Say Yes and Sign Up!

When you find yourself in the middle of a pivot, sit down and take a good long look at who you were, and who you want to become. And then...

• Write out the qualities you exude when you're at your finest. Think about when you are in flow; time is flying and you feel all buzzy with excitement because you just KNOW you're being your best self.

• Write down the qualities of the person you'd like to be and start putting together a plan of action for how to incorporate them into your life.

• Write down some hobbies, activities, and extracurriculars you'd love to try or see yourself doing in the future.

• Figure out the steps needed to make these things happen. Can you sign up for a sports team? Call up the friend you want to create art with? Sign up for a class?

• Once you know the steps, DO IT! Make it happen and put it on your calendar no matter how nervous or uncomfortable you may be.

"Tomorrow is always fresh, with no mistakes in it."

~ Lucy Maud Montgomery, Anne of Green Gables

Chapter Seven:
Pivoting in Your Career

Like everything else in life, career changes are inevitable. Otherwise, I would still be working at Pizza Hut for $2.13 an hour and a crapload of free breadsticks. Most people have no clue what they want to be when they grow up or they rarely stick with their original plan. We learn, we grow, we discover new passions or realize we're terrible at others, and we keep changing it up as we pivot. And, sometimes, the pivot is made for us.

As a kid, I was a big believer that, "If you just put your mind to it, you can do anything." I figured if I concentrated hard enough, I could be an olympic gymnast. However, I didn't consider that I'd not only have to work my butt off, but I'd also have to have some sort of natural ability to make that happen. Simply pinning magazine photos to a poster board wouldn't magically turn me into a gold medal winning olympian. Not to mention that as a 5'6", fully-developed 10-year-old, I never stood a chance as a gymnast.

My ever-supportive parents helped me to build a "gym" in our basement, complete with a balance beam and a mattress to practice on. I'd spend hours each day down there...practicing my cool gymnastics walk and my post-competition interviews with various imaginary news outlets. Maybe, just maybe, I was more interested in being the center of attention than I was in exhibiting any athletic prowess.

In middle school, for take-your-daughter-to-work day, I asked my mom if I could shadow someone at our big local theater, The Wharton Center, and be their "pretend kid" for the day. There was a moment at the end of my tour when I was standing on stage looking at over 2,000 empty chairs, when a crew member started working on the spotlight for an upcoming show; the moment the light hit me, I knew, this was where I belonged.

By high school, there was something about being on a stage in front of others that just always fired me up. The live audience and the thrill of not knowing what would happen next, excited me. Would it be an award-winning moment or an epic fail? I loved every bit of it and felt so alive there.

Where that would take me, of course, I had no clue. My dreams went from being cast on Saturday Night Live, to Broadway, to becoming a country music singer, to trying my hand at acting in Los Angeles.

Learn to Go With the Flow

One of my biggest growing experiences came when I worked at the Double JJ Resort in Rothbury, Michigan during my summers at college. I went as a studious musical theater major, ready to perform on stage, wowing audiences everywhere. Soon after arriving, I realized that this was more of a Cancun for 40-year-old cowboy wannabes, and families looking to camp and check out a petting zoo, than it was a place to be "discovered". I was thrown into stunt shows, improv and sketch comedy shows, party-perking (a fancy word for standing on stage and pouring shots into peoples mouths), and even riding a bull while singing the national anthem at rodeos. I would have my script perfectly memorized and blocked out, only to have my boss go off the cuff, making up his own dialogue mid-show. Thus I was forced to listen, react, and go with it. It was the greatest experience of learning to adapt and go with the flow. I became a better actor, entertainer, and overall better human by being forced to put down the script, be fully present, and learn to have fun!

One of my favorite life lessons came in the form of two 60-pound speakers on an extremely hot summer day. My boss took me to the rodeo arena and told me I had to get each speaker up the 20 foot ladder and into the speaker boxes. Now, I use the term "ladder" loosely here; they were tiny blocks of wood nailed into the beam all the way up. I looked at him and said, "There's no way. That's impossible. I can barely lift these speakers, let alone carry them up this ladder." He replied, "You'll figure it out. See you at lunch!"

And that was that. I had no choice but to figure out a way to get it done – and I did.

I think back on that moment a lot when something comes up in life that feels utterly impossible. "You'll figure it out." And I always do. A lot of things seem impossible until they're done. Moving forward each day in the midst of grief, getting back out there after rejection, trying again after a business goes under. You'll figure it out. Or as New York Times bestselling author and entrepreneur Marie Forleo says, *Everything is Figureoutable*.

While at the Double JJ, I met a guy from England who became my boyfriend. After our summers working together were over, we continued to date long-distance. I'd make trips to visit him and travel around Europe while I was there. After college, I went to live in England for six months and spent three weeks backpacking around Europe. This was the kind of unplanned awesome pivot that life is truly all about!

But when I realized that my loud, beer-drinking American side didn't quite fit in with becoming a proper British housewife, we decided to end our relationship. We had one more summer planned at the Double JJ together and decided that, at the end of the summer, we would go our separate ways. But not before he bought a one-way ticket from Nashville back to England. He also bought me a guitar and said, "If we're not going to have a future together, you have to at least go after your dreams. So, you're going to need to either drive nine hours to Tennessee to take me to the airport, or move there in the fall and pursue this music thing."

Trust the Unexpected Divine

This brings me to a good point. Sometimes our life pivots come to us in more of a God-shouting, "SURPRISE! You're going this way now!" kinda way. Yes, we still have the option to say "no," but I usually figure if it's that obvious I should go here, I should probably go here!

After moving to Nashville, my old Double JJ line dancing skills (another random job I was thrown into while working there) came in handy as I became a line dance instructor and emcee at the Wildhorse Saloon. The best part about scoring that job was that I can't dance to save my life! I'm 100% sure I was hired entirely for the fact that I had NO shame and could get hundreds of tourists up and doing a running man dance-off in no time. I had an ex once tell me that, when I dance, I look like the inflatable air dancing men at car lots – honestly, he was pretty spot on.

Long story short (well, still pretty long), line dancing brought me into music videos, which took me back to acting, which turned into looking at a potential move to Los Angeles. While I had no desire to live in California, seeing the mountains there during a quick trip made me rethink it. But I still wasn't entirely sold.

After returning from my trip, I was still working at the Wildhorse Saloon when a tourist and I were talking in the bathroom. It turned out she was an agent in Los Angeles who LOVED Nashville and wanted to move there. I explained that I was looking into moving to L.A. and she gave me her card. My heart nearly leapt into my throat when I saw her name.

"Um, you're the agent I've been sending my headshots and resume to," I said. We kept in touch, and a little while later she asked if I wanted to move and sublease my place to her, and she got me an audition with the agency. Again, I wasn't really planning on moving quite yet...but when the universe delivers this kind of fate moment, you gotta grab it.

If you're open to it, the universe (God) will send you signs for the directions you're supposed to go. I suggest you listen.

After a couple of years in Los Angeles, I was drained. I enjoyed being on set but it still felt like a job to me. At the end of the day, I was left still wondering if I'd be home in time to watch *The Bachelor*. Not the kind of fire I thought acting would bring me. I missed being on stage. I felt like such a failure. What now? How do I pivot AGAIN?!?

Figure Out What Fuels You and Do More of That!

It was at this time that I started reading the book that truly changed my life. It's called *You Are A Badass* by Jen Sincero. I suggest you pick it up, read it 85 times, highlight it, and memorize it; this book is life! In it, Sincero writes, "If time and money weren't a factor, what would you be doing? Do more of that!"

This book also got me thinking about where I was my happiest, best self, and fully in the flow of things when time didn't seem to exist. On stage. It had always been on stage. Going all the way back to when I pretended to do interviews in my basement, the moment the spotlight hit me on stage, and when I hosted at Stagecoach Country Music Festival. There is nothing better than being on stage dancing with thousands of people, riffing with drunk guests, killing time improv'ing in between announcing acts; it's heaven for me. My big "aha! moment" hit me like lightning. I wanted to be a host, an emcee, an entertainer, anything that would give me more stage time. My travel show was born.

Sometimes when we hit these pivotal moments in our lives, especially in our careers, it's easy to feel like we're failing, we're behind, or that we're lost. I believe that we're only truly lost if we give up, settle, and chase money because we're too scared to take a chance, start over, and potentially live the badass kind of life we know we want. Most times when it seems like things are falling apart, they're actually falling into place.

It's never too late to start over and pivot. Even if you have your dream career at 18, chances are as you get older, your goals and what you consider a "dream career" will change. It might be in the same industry but we should always be growing and seeking out what brings us the most joy. I've always wanted to be an entertainer and that's taken a ton of different forms. The changing pivot always felt like I was giving up, exhausted, unmotivated, and lost…but then it would hit me, BOOM! I should try this now!!!

A few examples of success if you're feeling behind…

- Stan Lee created his first hit comic book in 1961 at the age of 39.

- Joy Behar didn't launch her show business career until after the age of 40 after spending years as a high school English teacher.

- Vera Wang was a fashion editor and figure skater before deciding at age 40 to start designing wedding dresses.

- Alan Rickman was 41 when he landed his first big movie role in *Die Hard*.

- Martha Stewart worked on Wall Street before she wrote her first book at the age of 41 and launched *Martha Stewart Living*.

- Steve Carell didn't become a household name until he was 42 years old and starred as Michael Scott in *The Office*.

- Henry Ford was 45 when he created the Model T car.

- Samuel L. Jackson was a recovering addict when he scored his breakout role in "*Pulp Fiction*" at the age of 46.

- Charles Darwin was 50 years old when he published his famous *On the Origin of the Species.*

- Julia Child wrote her first cookbook at 39 years old and began hosting *The French Chef* at 51.

- Arianna Huffington started *The Huffington Post* at 55.

- Laura Ingalls Wilder published the first *Little House* book at 65.

Remember: It's NEVER too late to pivot, chase your passions, or make a career change.

It's Ok To Step Back and Reevaluate Your Goals

As I am writing this book, I'm in the process of moving from Los Angeles after 10 years, to start a life with someone I've just met, in Denver, Colorado. Why? Because every part of me says this is the right next step! When Coronavirus hit and quarantine began, I was forced to take a break from my travel show *Monica Goes*. This step back helped me realize that, as much as I loved being on camera, I missed the stage and needed to find a new way to balance both.

When I decided to stop for a couple of months, I was a mess! I remember walking with my fellow entrepreneurial neighbor and telling him, "I've put out a video every two weeks for almost six years, I can't just stop!!!" To which he asked, "Why? What would happen if you did?" He reminded me that taking a pause is not quitting. Especially when it gives your heart and brain the space to step back and ask, "What do I REALLY want?"

In the month since I've stopped producing content for the sake of my timeline and what I thought I **should** be doing (stupid "should"!) I created a new plan for my travel show, came up with the concept for a new show to start in Denver that fires me up, and wrote this book that you're reading now!

Sometimes what we think of as a setback is actually a set up that will drive us further, faster, and help us refuel our passion for what we truly love. And if you're in those moments in between careers and hitting burnout, take a moment to breathe, reset, and know that this is an incredible time to pivot.

How to Figure Out What To Do With Your Life

That's not a big ol' question or anything! I think growing up I always believed this was a one and done question. "Oh, doctor! Got it. That's my life. Ok, bye!" But the truth is that the average person changes careers 4-7 times in their lifetime…and if you're an entrepreneur and/or creative, I'm gonna guess that it's more like 82 times. But don't quote me on that!

I believe figuring out what you want to do in life is more about figuring out what brings you the most joy and helps you feel like your best self NOW.

Then, learning how to make money at that and figuring out how to do it as often as possible. After that, it's all about being open to how that may shift over time and learning to go with the flow.

As someone who has been in the career pivot phase many, MANY times, the next exercise will provide you with some questions I ask when I find myself there.

Exercise Time:
What Career is Best For You?

*Tip: Journal this out and allow yourself the freedom to write and see what you come up with. Studies show that actually putting pen to paper helps us to dive deeper into our thoughts and really internalize what we are writing.

Questions to ask yourself:

- If money wasn't a factor, what would I want to be doing?

- If I had all the time in the world, what would I work on?

- What kinds of jobs do I find myself being drawn to?

- What do I find myself talking about all of the time? (For me, I'm ALWAYS talking about pivoting and once I realized that, BOOM I had my book idea!)

- What am I doing when I seem to lose sense of time because I'm just in the flow of it?

• F.L.O.W - Feel like ourselves, winning! I just made that up but it kinda works, right? Flow is the state you're in when things come naturally, you lose time, and you're happy because the task at hand is something you mindlessly love.

Things to do:

• Create a vision board (we'll talk more about that later) and see what kinds of things you're naturally drawn to to add to it.

• Ask (and LISTEN!) for signs of what pivots you should make.

• Ask five friends what qualities they love about you and what you're great at. You might be surprised at what they say! Don't ask them what they see you doing...try to tap into what you're already doing naturally and see if you can find a way to make money at that.

Let's get one thing straight: NO ONE has it all figured out. And if they say they do, they're lying (and probably super unhappy deep down but that's for them to figure out). So many of us are under the impression that we should know who we are and what we want to be by the age of 18, or at least by the time we have a degree in something that we may not even want to do in the first place.

Life changes, people change, careers change, and it's all normal! Stop feeling like you're behind if you are starting over. Stop feeling lost if you're in the middle of a pivot. And stop comparing yourself to everyone around you (they're lost too, I promise). Give yourself a break, take a breath, and lean into the pivot!

"Behind every successful man there's a lot of unsuccessful years."

~ Bob Brown

Chapter Eight:
The Woo-Woo Stuff
That'll Change Your Life

I'll start this chapter by saying that God can mean different things to different people; The Universe, Jesus Christ, Buddha, Energy, whatever you believe or want to call it. I personally believe they're all the same. Because of my own beliefs and experiences, I refer to Him as the Christian "God." And if you're not religious, there's some good stuff in this chapter for you too. I want to gently encourage you to give this faith stuff a go because it may change your life and it will certainly make it a heck of a lot more peaceful!

My Faith Journey

Growing up Catholic I had some big questions (and still do); I was pretty skeptical of the whole thing. My first big "Whoa, is this for real?" kinda moment was when I was 8 years old. My mom really wanted me to play the piano but I really wanted to do ballet instead. After three years of keyboard lessons, I was miserable. I remember one particular night, I was so frustrated that I got down on my knees and sobbed, "Please, please don't make me play the keyboard anymore." About five minutes later, my mom came back upstairs and, out of nowhere said, "You don't have to take keyboard lessons anymore." Whoa!

But after years of dabbling here and there in churches, nature was always where I felt closest to God. Something about seeing with my own two eyes all of the magnificent things He created, and realizing the world was so much bigger than whatever teenage girl problem I was dealing with, helped me to feel connected.

During the tumultuous years of my marriage, I started working harder and harder at my faith. I was reading every book I could about how to make my marriage work, and going to couples counseling alone. I even hid a bible under the mattress on my ex's side of the bed to try to somehow get it to magically absorb through his skin. All it did was give him back problems. I didn't know what I was trying for but I knew I needed a miracle.

Even after finding a church that I loved, the Catholic in me still wasn't all about the hug-your-neighbor and chat about life just yet. I was more of a "sneak in five minutes late and aim for the balcony where no one can see you" kinda Christian.

One Sunday, I was feeling particularly hopeless. Like every other week, the service ended with, "If anyone would like some extra prayer, there will be deacons up front to pray with you." Out of nowhere I felt my feet walking me down the aisle toward these strangers. Two deacons laid their hands on me and prayed for my marriage and a sense of peace. On the way home, I started bawling hysterically. And I'm talking the kind of "I can't breathe, hyperventilating" type of sobbing. Then, I felt something super weird. It was like a warm glow and goosebumps all at the same time and everything started to go white. I pulled the car over because I wasn't sure if I was going to pass out or what! Afterward, I felt this rush of peace come over me. From that day on, through all of the continued arguments, I never quite felt rage again. I felt peace. I still wasn't entirely sure about all this woo-woo stuff, but I did know 100% that that was God.

As things continued to decline in my marriage, I was really becoming hopeless. My ex no longer wanted kids, or a dog, or a house, and I felt so incredibly trapped. The life I thought I had signed up for was no longer an option. One Sunday in church, I started feeling that wooshy, goosebumpy, warm feeling again and internally remembered thinking, "Oh good, God, you're here! Now tell me what to do!" The second I thought about it, the feeling started to disappear. "Wait!," I screamed in my head. And then, no joke, I freaking HEARD God. Yep, I'm one of THOSE people now... but I swear I did.

And He said, "Relax, you'll know soon enough." After the service, I was saying hello to a lady in church and she just took me in a big hug and said, "It's ok, you can let go. You've done enough." One week later, my ex confessed to cheating.

The biggest thing I've learned in my newish Christian journey is that it's really about creating a relationship with God and being a good human. It makes me angry when so-called Christians become judgmental about what's right and wrong with other people when the entire point is to show, live, and be love. I was put off of religion for YEARS by "These people are going to Hell" kinda Christians. I even told one girl, "It's a good thing you're not St. Peter because no one would be getting in on your watch." These people had missed the whole point. I became more interested in Christianity when a girl I once worked with was ALWAYS calm, smiling, and glowy. I asked her what her secret was and she simply said, "My faith." And I thought, "Oooh I want some of that stuff if that's what it looks like." THAT'S living a Christian life.

I remember realizing faith was a relationship with God when I was just filled with anger at the way my life was going. Like inner rage, furious, I'm-gonna-punch-a-wall kinda anger. I was trying to "pray" and "keep the faith" when my good southern friend told me, "Girl, sounds like you just need to hash it out with Jesus." And I remember thinking, "Whoa, I can do that?" So I did! I screamed, I yelled, I swore, and I felt closer to God than all of my praying and trying to see the best in things ever made me feel. God doesn't want perfect; He wants YOU. In whatever form that means.

And I learned a long time ago that I'm pretty sure God has a REALLY good sense of humor! I mean, he made me this weird, crazy, outgoing person who now talks about "God." What! Who am I? I was so put off by the seemingly perfect Christian girls for years. I figure maybe God wants to use my attention-loving, loud mouth, beer-drinking craziness to reach those people in between. I mean, if one person can think, "Man, if that girl goes to church maybe I can see what it's all about," then I'm doing something right. I even debated writing a raunchy stand up comedy special and calling it "Holy Shit." I think God would approve.

All of this is to say that if religion puts you off, I GET it! If bible-thumping weirdos with picket signs of damnation make you wanna throw up a middle finger and run away, I GET it! That's not faith to me. God loves you as you are and just wants to hang, that's all. It's as simple as that. Oh, and maybe be a good human so someone else can say, "Hey, how do I get some of that feel good juju?" If you've been put off before, maybe give it another go with some other chill people who camp, drink, and think stars are cool. And then go from there.

How Does Faith Help You Pivot?

Ok, so now that we're through the whole churchy part of the chapter, let me tell you WHY this stuff is so helpful with pivoting and with life in general. Remember that whole chapter on anxiety and depression? There are TONS of great verses and songs that can help you to get through those feelings. Here are a few of my favorites:

> *"Who of you by worrying can add a single hour to his life?" Luke 12:25*

"Therefore do not worry about tomorrow, for tomorrow will worry about itself. Each day has enough trouble of its own." Matthew 6:34

"Cast all of your anxieties on Him because he cares for you." 1 Peter 5:7

See? There's some good stuff in there, I promise! Having faith and knowing that God has a plan for you also helps create a sense of calm amidst the chaos of life's changes. After my whole, "Whoa God, was that you?" moment in church, I remember having a complete sense of calm during the crazy few months that followed after leaving my marriage. Even to the point where my atheist ex said, "Wow, I kinda get that whole God thing, seeing how calm you are now."

But while I believe God does have a plan and an ideal end-goal, we still have to make our own choices. I don't believe that when I was born God was like, "That one, she's got divorce written all over her!" I think life is more like a *Choose Your Own Adventure* book and God just kinda changes the outcome depending on what path we choose. But, ultimately, the ending is the same. I think when I ignored my gut and decided, yep, I'm gonna go through with this whole crap-marriage thing, God was like, "Welp, ok...not the choice I would have advised but, hey, I can work with this. It's gonna take you a long way around for the final goal but I'll put some good lessons in there for ya!" And He did. If you listen, they will come.

I mean that kinda worked, right? God really does like to chat and I think the more we ask and listen, the more we can hear Him. But even now I struggle to really tap in and get that ol' goosebumpy feeling again. And that's because life and our own thoughts get in the way. But I believe if we work on our relationship with God/The Universe/Energy – whatever you wanna call it – we can learn to take the correct pivots more often.

I once heard a speaker say, "When we pray, we talk. When we meditate, we listen." I realized I was doing a lot of talking without actually listening for an answer. I started to give myself 30 minutes each morning. Ten minutes of bible study and prayer, ten minutes of meditating on what I just read and listening to hear what God had to say, and then ten minutes of journaling to write about what I had learned. This simple routine started getting me more accustomed to building a relationship with God rather than just saying, "Hey bro, I need this. Cool thanks, bye!"

Meditation and Tapping Into the Good Stuff

Meditation is good for SO many reasons. And I say this as a newbie – not one of those, "I have a meditation room where I hang out for three hours with my shaman" kinda people. Here are some of the things I notice when I give myself 10 minutes of meditation in the morning:

Meditation Mornings	Non Meditation Mornings
I feel calm, less anxious.	I am super anxious.
I have more time, and get more done.	I feel like I'm behind all day.
I have a sense of purpose.	I am just working to work.
I'm happier around others.	People annoy me more easily.
I have a lot more energy.	I am super tired.

As a total novice, some days I set my alarm for 10 minutes and just keep repeating a word like "focus" or "listen" and try to quiet my brain.

Other days, the wheels are just cranking, so I'll pull up a 10-minute meditation on YouTube or from an app that's about whatever I'm seeking that day.

You can search "10 Minute Meditation to Help Productivity/Positivity/Relationships", etc. I've also heard it's really helpful to set an intention for the day and meditate on that.

However you do it, I find my to-do list gets done twice as fast, and I'm just in a better headspace, if I give myself 10 minutes each morning to get focused.

I really can't recommend it enough!

Exercise Time:
Give it a Go!

• Set a timer - start with 5 or 10 minutes and go from there.

• Sit in a quiet, comfortable position. (Most people say cross-legged but if that's not comfortable for you just make sure you're sitting upright somewhere.)

• Set your hands on your knees.

• Palms up invites energy into your body.

• Palms down helps calm an anxious mind.

• Close your eyes and focus on your breath.

• Set an intention for either your meditation time, or for the entire day.

• Focus on quieting your mind and your thoughts.

• Try this in silence one day, a guided meditation the next, music another day. Play around and see what works best for you.

- After the timer goes off, gently open your eyes, wiggle your fingers and toes, and slowly stretch as you ease into your day.

Manifestation and Actually Making it Happen

I feel like we all have that one friend who watched *The Secret*, went all in on manifesting stuff, and it all just started to appear for them. Well, if you're like me, instead of thinking, "Oooh, I wanna do that too", you thought "Ewww, that's so new age and hippie dippy. Good for her but I'm gonna go be 'cool' and chug a beer with the boys." No? Just me? Well, it's taken me many years of living in Los Angeles and lots of woo-woo friends to dip my toe into the whole "picture it and it's yours" world...but I have to admit, it's kinda awesome. There are a few incredible benefits to this practice.

When I started reading book after book which talked about "picturing your dream life", I realized there may be something to this. I learned to combine the whole "sit down and visualize it" technique with the realist in me that needs steps and to-do lists to make things happen. Here's how it works:

Remember the exercise from Chapter 2 about visualizing your best life? Let's go over it again. Sit down and close your eyes. Start picturing your life in five or ten years. Get really specific. Run through the day-to-day.

I start with picturing my life from the moment my alarm goes off. Who's next to me? What does the bed feel like? What does the room look like? What is the first thing I get up to do? What are the sounds I hear? And then I go from there, working out my daily routine of this dream life.

I get up, kiss my husband, run six miles, shower, have my morning time (bible study, meditation, and journaling), and then wake up my kid. Laughing, so much laughing. Head to the home office and go over my schedule for the day; setting up speaking engagements, travel shoots, writing, whatever it is. Meet with my assistant and producer working on my dream jobs. Etc. Etc. Etc.

I get SOOOO specific about what my house looks like, what my office looks like, and then how everything feels. The sense of peace and accomplishment.

The excitement for upcoming projects. The love for my family and team. After I've gone through every detail, I open my eyes and write out exactly what I pictured.

Exercise Time (Again!):
Make a Plan of Action

Here's the part that makes me feel like it's ACTUALLY going to happen. I don't just send out good vibes and wishes into the universe and then go about my life. I work it backward into a typical daily schedule. An example might look like this:

5 years	1 year`	1 month	This week
Run 6 miles	Run 3 miles	Run 2 miles	Run 1 mile
Have a kid	Relationship	Meet someone	Go on two dates
Emmy for show	Show on network	Three network meetings	Create pitch

Obviously, this will look different for everyone depending on your goals. Having giant goals is great but it can be super overwhelming. If in your dream scenario you have a smokin' hot bod but in reality you need to lose 50 lbs., that can feel impossible. But if you break it down to, "Whoa, if I lose 2 lbs. a month, I'll be there in just over two years!" it can feel pretty doable. And then create an ACTUAL plan of HOW to do it.

When I started training for my marathon, I couldn't even run a mile! I worked back each week of training to figure out the amount of time I'd need to get there and then started with 1/2 mile runs 3x a week and one 1-mile run. And then I took my sweet, sweet time to build up. That's how you make the dream life actually happen.

Start living mini versions of your ideal life today on a small scale. If in my dream life I get up and casually run eight miles in the morning, maybe now I'll start waking up and casually run one. Once it becomes routine, you can build on that. Before you know it, your dream self is just what comes naturally because you've already put the steps into place.

Turning my "manifestations" into an actionable to-do list was the quickest way for me to see change, and help me feel less hippieish.

The Power of a Vision Board

When I first read *The Secret* and read about vision boards, I wasn't fully signing up for the whole "I put a picture of a house on a piece of cardboard and the next year I bought that exact house!" kinda thing. But in the same way that there is power in physically writing down the things you want, there is power in actually seeing them as well.

Since getting on board with the whole vision board (see what I did there) phenomenon, I have heard more and more stories of people manifesting the things they cut out from a magazine into their real life. In fact, just yesterday, I realized I had put my favorite hiking boot brand on my vision board at the beginning of this year (a brand I've been trying to work with for six years) and they emailed me last week to ask if they could send me some boots! Say what?!? If for nothing else, every time I create a vision board it forces me to step back, reconsider the things I want in life and, if necessary, pivot!

What is a vision board?

In the same way meditation and journaling can help you to mentally picture the future you want, a vision board is a way of transferring what you see in your mind into a tangible visual representation. Think of it as a Pinterest page for your life!

How To Create One

Creating a vision board can be done in a few different ways. The most basic is to flip through magazines and cut out pictures and words that grab your attention. Then paste them to a poster board, foam board, or even just a blank sheet of paper. I really like to have a meditation session or do the previous visualization exercise beforehand and THEN go through images to see what fits with the things I desire to go on the board. I've seen some people segment their boards to include different sections for "Life", "Career", "Family", etc.

Other ways include writing down the things you want on the board, printing out fake news stories about what you want to happen, drawing photos, or whatever it is that inspires you and brings you closer to the goals you desire.

For my latest vision board, I put all of these together. First, I went out and bought magazines that I knew would have images that spoke to me. These included Backpacker, Women's Health, Better Homes and Gardens, Colorado Lifestyle, Trail Running, etc. In the past, I just used whatever free magazines I could find but then I wasn't as intentional about the images I was using.

Next, I meditated for 10 minutes and pictured the ideal life and the things I looked around and saw in my mind. Then I started flipping through the magazines and cutting out any images or words that fit with the dream life I'd just pictured. I split my board into quadrants: "Career, Lifestyle and Fitness", "Home and Family", and the "Outdoors". Finally, I googled images for what I couldn't find in magazines (writing a book, speaking to a large audience at an event, becoming an on-camera travel host, etc.). Then I added these on my vision board as well. This was my way of ensuring the goals I had for myself were properly represented on the board.

My vision boards have changed many times over the years to fit what I'm looking to create more of in my life, in that particular season. Sometimes when we reach those pivotal moments, looking through magazines, Pinterest, and photos online or on Instagram can help us to determine what is standing out to us and why.

Then you can do some internal digging to see if that's a direction or goal you're feeling in your heart at the moment.

When Is the Best Time to Create A Vision Board?

Any time is a good time to create a vision board! But there are some times in our lives I feel it's more valuable and necessary. Again, not every board needs to be a well-planned out 20x20 masterpiece.

I've done some on a regular ol' 8 1/2 x 11 blank piece of paper because I felt inspired (or not inspired and looking for help).

Here are my go-to times for creating new vision boards.

~ New Years ~

I am a total nerd about New Years. It's not about the partying or the fancy outfits for me. I love that, globally, there's this sense of hope and new beginnings. People are setting goals, letting go of the past year, and getting excited about possibilities. Even if 99% of people are done with their resolutions by February, it's this brief moment in time when people see the best for their futures.

I plan the whole thing out! I've made resolutions since 1995 and consult back on them every year. To me it's not so much about a complete life overhaul and beating myself up for the things I didn't do, but more a way to keep track of my progress, check in that I'm still growing, and celebrate each win. It's awesome to see how far I've come; sometimes I look back on the things I thought I wanted and have a good laugh. In the words of Garth Brooks "Sometimes I thank God, for unanswered prayers."

I go through the previous year's list with two pens; red pen to cross out the goals that didn't get completed (if applicable they go on to the new year's list) and a blue pen to add a smiley face next to the ones that did. Then, I work on my new list and add any new goals I might have.

In the same way, this is an excellent time to create a vision board for the upcoming year. Especially if you're more of a short-term thinker and the idea of throwing up a picture of four kids on the board sends you into a panic attack. It's a good way to align yourself with the things you want to work on.

Then the important part: make a plan! Just like manifesting, you can't just throw up a million dollar home onto a piece of cardboard and then simply wait for it to come as you max out all of your credit cards.

~ Your Birthday ~

My friend Jeannette, who teaches vision board workshops and is sort of a master of manifestation, once told me, "Your birthday is your own personal New Year." Whether you believe in astrology and all the stars and moon ideologies, there is certainly a special energy around the day you were born.

Like New Years, this is a great time to reflect back on the previous year and make goals for your next year around the sun. The biggest thing I will say is this: Whatever you do, DON'T beat yourself up for not being where you thought you would be by X age or by comparing yourself to your friends who are your age and have accomplished this, this, and this. Remember what I said about the word "**should**." Throw it out of your vocabulary!!! Thinking I **should** be married, and have a house, and 2.5 kids by now, doesn't help anything.

It only discredits the totally awesome things you've done with your life – the things that "Sally the soccer mom" never got the chance to do! If you **should** have done that, you would have. Any other alternate universe where you did, doesn't exist. Let it go.

~ In The Pivot ~

When your life hits a major crossroad, this is the PERFECT time to step back and figure out where you want it to go from here. A vision board can be a great way to step into that new life. Keeping the old board up with your old life goals won't serve you any longer. Be thankful for the guidance that your past goals provided and get excited about your new and awesome life!

Any time you're moving, making a career change, ending a relationship, starting a new one, come into some money – whatever it may be – having a visual for 'what now?' can help take the fear out of these moments. Maybe "single me" had an awesome board filled with travel, hanging out with my girlfriends, and solo adventures. But now I'm ready to make one that includes a partner and kids, and perhaps a career change.

Maybe you lived in a big city by a lake but now you're moving to the rural mountains. The urban nightlife and boating images might change to hiking and enjoying a slower pace of life. Anything you can do to help turn your anxious fear of change into optimistic enthusiasm is a great step in the right direction.

What to do with your Vision Board?

The final thing I'll say about vision boards, is now that you've created it, put it somewhere where you'll see it every day. This one was actually difficult for me for the longest time! I was so embarrassed to have a photo of $1,000,000 on my living room wall. What would my friends think?!? Or the images of a husband and kids...that's gonna be awkward for someone I just started dating. Look, unless you printed off 18 images of HIM from his Instagram page, it's totally normal to display the things you want in life without being creepy.

Don't be ashamed of your goals because then you're just telling yourself that you don't believe you deserve to have them, which defeats the whole purpose! Put it in your bedroom or your office if you're not super comfortable with it in the living room, but make sure you see it every day. Subconsciously, the images will remind you of what you're working toward. Plus, they're pretty!

Exercise Time:
You Guessed it... Make Your Own Vision Board!

Have fun and feel free to use the examples I've outlined in this chapter. Your vision board can be an actual board, a scrapbook, a corkboard– whatever works best for you!

"Don't wait for the right opportunity. Create it."

~ George Bernard Shaw

Chapter Nine:
A Global Shift

Every now and again the world shifts and everyone seems to be pivoting at the same time. To say this can (and most likely will) create anxiety and big life changes is an understatement. This may be something that affects a small group of people and is local or the entire world heading into a big ol' shit storm.

You know that feeling you get when you're in a great mood but Negative Nancy comes around with her complaining and pessimism and before you know it your mood is ruined too? Well, it's kind of like that, but everything and everyone around you is that person! Hold on tight because it's rough! Here are some examples:

Small Scale Shifts

- You move and suddenly need to pivot your career, friends, favorite coffee shop, etc.

- Your kids school gets a new principal and policies change.

- The church changes pastors/affiliations, etc.

- The CEO of your company changes which has a trickle-down effect on the entire business.

- Your city or state has a natural disaster or crisis happen.

- Protests and movements affect your city or state.

- Your state or country has new elected officials which changes things.

Big Ol' Shit Storm Shifts

- Natural disasters affecting large areas.

- Terrorism.

- Civil rights movement.

- Global pandemic.

- National election.

- Basically all of 2020.

These kinds of pivots are extremely trying because not only are they affecting your life personally, but the entire energy of those around you changes as well. As I write this, I am currently in quarantine during a global pandemic, amidst an election year and a global civil rights movement. To say the mood is heavy right now is stating it lightly.

Then, add in my own personal life shifts of changing careers, moving states, and beginning a new relationship and there are a LOT of emotions happening. There are a few different ways all of this can take place.

When Global Shifts are Bad but Personal Pivots are Good

Now for me, thank goodness, my personal pivots have mostly been good ones at the moment and, while extremely exciting, combined with all of the heaviness of the global shifts, it can be tough to balance the rollercoaster of emotions. Here's what this may look like:

- One day you're on top of the world with anticipation of positive changes and then the next day you're angry at the political climate and being quarantined. Actually, make that emotions shiftings every hour or so...

- Feeling guilty for being happy amidst so much despair.

- Trying to learn and grow while also being exhausted by so much change.

- Having so much to do and no motivation to do it.

When Global Shifts are Bad and Personal Pivots Also Suck

When I look around and see the world changing and feel the low energy of everything around me, I can't begin to imagine those who are also going through personal crises at the same time. Here are the ways that may look:

- Global pandemic, job loss, anxiety of finances all at once.

- Depression and being unmotivated and unexcited about the future.

- A feeling of hopelessness or loss of purpose.

- Relationship struggles or divorce during a global crisis.

- Loss of a loved one during a global crisis.

- Loss of a loved one due to the global crisis.

- Not getting the love and support you need personally because everyone is affected by this worldwide pivot at once.

All of these things combined lead to an incredibly intense time and I will say it again and again: IT'S OK TO NOT BE OK! The unexpected, uncontrollable disasters like this are awful for so many reasons but the main one is: no one saw it coming.

You couldn't have planned for that big tornado to take out your house; you never saw the world being this divided; and who could have guessed the entire world would go into quarantine? So, what do you do during this time? How do you get through it? Some days it's all about coming out on top and being your best self, and other times it's just getting through the day one minute at a time. Either way, that's ok! There is no right answer, because in most of these situations, it's all uncharted territory. Here are some of the things I've learned so far during this global shift.

There's no right way or wrong way to get through, you just have to get through it.

When the quarantine originally began I think a lot of us felt like, Ok, this is the time to write a book, learn a language, build my business, etc. etc. etc. But the truth is, we're only human. Once those human emotions of feeling as though the world is crashing in around you (because the news literally says it IS) kick in, it's hard to get motivated about increasing your social media following or starting a new hobby.

While it's great to have goals and see this time as an opportunity to propel forward, it's more important to be kind to yourself and also take the time you need to just be ok (or not be ok). Some days you may wake up motivated as hell, inspired to change the world, and ready to kill it in your career! Other days, the heavy energy might just be so overwhelming it takes all of your might not to stay in bed and open a bottle of wine at 10 a.m. It's ok. Honor whatever it is you are feeling that day. Just be mindful of your mental health as well. Make sure you're not having too many heavy days in a row without seeking help.

Don't compare how others are dealing with the crisis to how you are.

One of the strangest things about a global crisis is that everyone is dealing with the SAME problems but in their own individual ways. Some people go into action mode, jumping into altruistic behavior, volunteering, thriving in their career, seizing the moment, and soaring past your progress. That can feel like a LOT! On top of whatever it is you're already feeling! It's hard not to feel like you're getting left behind, or guilty for just not being ok in the moment...and you know what that does? A whole lotta nothing! That guilt and shame just pile on more negative emotions in a time when there's already enough of that.

Remember that what you see in others is what they WANT you to see, especially on social media! Perhaps they appear to be thriving and looking like a rock star, but after the camera turns off, they crawl back into bed and cry themselves to sleep. Not that you should wish that on anyone, but also don't compare your reality to someone else's highlight reel. We all deal with crises in our own ways. Some people come firing out of the gate and then crash and burn when their emotions catch up. Others are in a state of shock and can't seem to function and then finally wake up one day ready to make the shift and soar.

When the COVID-19 pandemic hit and quarantine began, I tried to jump at the opportunity of having more time. I started cranking out videos, going live on social media, and working on my website. About two weeks in, I realized that I had no actual motivation for any of this, my anxiety was through the roof, and I was burnt out.

So I stopped.

It was SOOOOO hard to watch friends of mine in the same field cranking out extra videos, getting guest spots on the news, and seemingly flying through the pandemic. But I KNEW if I kept going for the sake of keeping up, I wasn't going to come out any more motivated in my career.

I had consistently pushed out travel videos every two weeks for 5 1/2 years and the idea of stopping terrified me. It was my neighbor who reminded me "Pausing isn't quitting. It's simply resetting." He asked how I would feel if I stepped back and took a break. I said I'd feel relieved. So I paused. I took care of myself. I let myself feel and do whatever I wanted to feel and do that day. And you know what happened... I met an amazing guy, decided to move to Denver, came up with a new business plan for *Monica Goes* as well as a new travel show, and started writing a book. And I didn't lose a single follower.

Be careful what you let in.

Whenever there's a global crisis (or any crisis for that matter), the world is ready to spew all of the negative, horrible things happening and shove them down your throat until you're convinced there's no point in going on. The news, social media, that one friend who assumes the worst, all of it starts worming its way into your world until even the strongest of people start to crumble. Stay informed but know when to turn it off.

This is especially important if you are an empath. Empathic people FEEL the pain of others. If you continuously let the energy of the world (which, during a crisis, is super, super low) affect you, it's going to be an even harder time.

When the pandemic hit in 2020, I was tuning in day and night to hear the news, the number of infected, death toll, city plans, etc. I watched the morning news, the evening news, the daily White House briefings, and all 18 social media platforms. Sure enough, by month two, I was living in my pj's, doing puzzles, and indulging in a multitude of "Quarantini's".

I finally started changing up my routine. I made sure the FIRST thing I did in the morning was my bible study and meditation. It was most important to start the day positively and to remember Who's in charge, and that it's going to be ok. Then I would allow myself one morning show while I had breakfast to catch up.

I recommend the morning shows because they give you the facts while throwing in light-hearted stories and fashion trends, so it feels less heavy than the big news outlets. It's like decaf news. And that was it. Then I would get outside, read, and go about my day. If things got crazy I knew I'd have people blowing up my phone to let me know when I should tune back in. But it's important to have balance and know when to tune out and turn off.

Get Involved

If you're the type of person who needs to feel like you're moving forward but it's a time when you can't move forward like you used to, find another way to keep going. If there's a movement taking place, get involved. Ask how you can help. Donate. Volunteer. Take time to step back and learn, then dive in and help. Feeling like you're helping others and working toward progress can give you the motivation to keep going and some meaning in your life when your normal routine isn't an option. It's also been proven to boost your mood when you give back and help others. It can bring you out of the dark thoughts that may be swirling around in the ol' noggin.

Another way to get involved, while still being on your own, is to learn and grow. Not only was there a major pandemic in 2020, there was also a massive civil rights movement and worldwide protests going on for equal rights for people of color.

As someone who was immunocompromised, getting out and marching was too risky with the Coronavirus going on. So I took this time to LISTEN and grow.

I started watching documentaries and reading articles that talked about the struggles black people have faced in America. I have a long way to go and will never fully understand, but it was something that 1. Took me out of my own problems to see the bigger picture, 2. Helped me be more empathetic toward others and fueled a desire to learn more, and 3. Implanted new ideas and understanding that would last far longer than the quarantine.

Reach out to others and ask for help

When our entire world shifts, whether it be the loss of a loved one, the addition of a loved one, a global pandemic, or a natural disaster, nothing is the same anymore and we are forever changed. It can be easy to want to go within ourselves and shut down. While self-care days are amazing (and necessary), if you stay in that place too long it can have a massive negative impact on your psyche.

Now is the time to reach out to friends and family. Stay connected. So much of a global crisis is everyone going through the same thing but separately. Humans need humans. Sometimes you may reach out to someone because you feel the need to connect but don't realize they also needed that connection. I had someone tell me once, "When you don't go to church you deprive everyone of the opportunity to connect with you." I had never thought of it that way before. I just figured no one would notice. But it's the same with connecting to loved ones. When you don't reach out, it deprives them of the opportunity to connect to you as well. Whether it's church, work, or life in general, not showing up hurts others as much as it hurts you.

I hate to ask for help. I am independent to a fault and after my divorce, I never wanted to feel like I NEEDED anyone ever again. I didn't want to let people in because, in my mind, that made me weak. But the truth is, loving others is the bravest thing we can do! And in the same way as the church analogy, my "being strong independently" was depriving others of getting to know and love me as well.

Connecting with, and loving each other, is what we were put on this earth to do. When your world falls apart, it's much easier to move forward when you lean on one another. So don't be afraid to make the first move and reach out. We all want to feel understood and related to and when something happens to all of us at once, what better time to connect and help each other through?

Protect Your Energy

In the same way as if you had a lot of negative friends you'd eventually find yourself complaining all of the time as well, if you focus on the negative global crises you'll find yourself diving deep and indulging in hopeless daily thoughts. It's always important to protect your energy and be selective about who and what you're letting into your life. But it's especially crucial when people on a mass scale are in a low-energy state.

Be kind to yourself. Mourn your losses; people, things, time, dreams, whatever it may be. Let yourself grieve. Let yourself feel and honor whatever you're feeling that day. Take things one day at a time. Have faith and lean into knowing that there is a bigger plan that you may not see yet. Take time for yourself and also connect to others. Find a balance in your emotions. Stop comparing yourself to others. Know that it's ok to not be ok. As I once heard someone say, "This is not an apocalypse, it's an awakening."

"If you want to change the world, start with yourself."

~ Gandhi

Chapter Ten:
Create Your Best Life

There is no secret weapon to managing and getting through life's big pivots. The truth is, we're all doing the best we can with what we know. My biggest piece of advice through all of this is to BE KIND TO YOURSELF and know that IT'S OK TO NOT BE OK! That being said, here are some of the big things you can do when life pulls its giant rug out from underneath your feet.

When Your Career Goals Change (Or Are Changed For You)

First things first, take a deep breath. Remember, most people change careers many times throughout their life so ending, changing, and beginning a new career is NORMAL. You are NOT a failure, or behind, or unqualified, or whatever other lies you are telling yourself. You're brave, you're strong, and you've got this! Take it day by day. Remember, life is like a *Choose Your Own Adventure* book.

Figure out what this new goal and career look like for your life five years down the road and work it back into small chunks and goals that you can tackle now. Journal and do self-affirmations to remind yourself you're a badass and super qualified for this. The amount of times I was sure I had no business going out for a career only to realize by day two that I knew way more than I thought I did is unbelievable. Don't let your fear of the unknown stop you from putting yourself out there and going for it anyway.

When a Relationship Ends, Begins, or Changes - Thank the Universe

Relationship pivots are one of the hardest things to navigate simply because it doesn't involve just you! As a self proclaimed strong and independent woman, I feel confident about navigating changes in my own life and using the tools I've created and my motivation to carry me through. But when a relationship ends (or begins), so much of the change is out of my hands. I can be a bit of a control freak and when conversations and changes don't go the way I had them all mapped out to go in my mind; shifting against my will can be like trying to move a 200 lb. revolving door. Relationships are all about compromise and allowing changes to happen together while remaining independent people as well.

I've been guilty of both losing myself entirely in relationships trying to hold them together by doing and being whatever the other person wanted and, on the flip side, trying SO hard to maintain my independence that I'm stubborn and don't let the other person in at all.

It's ok to grow and change within a relationship. GROW is the key word; when it's a change that you like, that helps you become more of the person you want to be, it can be worth all of the uncomfortable emotions. When relationships end, there are two sides of pivoting. First, there's mourning the loss of the relationship and the life you thought you were going to be leading. You have to give yourself time to grieve and then, put it to rest. Next, there's figuring out who you are now and who you want to become and getting to the work of loving yourself again.

The quickest way to get to the second part and start loving yourself more is to forgive yourself. And forgive the other person as well. Remember, we're all human and just doing the best we can with what we know. Forgive them for your sake, leave it in love, and step forward into your new awesome life full of amazing possibilities.

Sometimes a relationship changes. You move, you have a kid, one person loses their job, etc. The key is to work through the changes together. Keep getting to know one another and stay kind. I once heard that a marriage is made up of a bunch of little relationships and marriages. It's constant change and getting to know one another all over again. Help each other create a new dream life outlook and figure out how the changes can help you to achieve that. Take things slow and move one step at a time. And do your best to enjoy all the moments, big and small, in the meantime.

Start Building Your Toolbox

As I mentioned in Chapter 4, one of the best ways to get through the mental hurdles of life's pivots, is to expect change. Have a tool kit of ways to get through it, and then trial and error until you find something that works for you. Being prepared can help you to feel more in control when things around you seem to be spinning out of control. And this isn't something you need to sit down and map out and have posted on a wall somewhere. This is for you and you only.

The easiest way to build the mental health tool kit is to start taking stock of things that feel really good to you. "Oh man, when I dance around like a moron blasting music, I feel like I can take on the world!" Ok, write it down. "Journaling helps me get a clearer idea of what's true and what is in my imagination." Ok, write it down. Slowly over time, you'll have a list of things that you know have been proven to help you stay positive when your world starts turning to shit and your brain follows.

Remember, the key is to stop the spiral BEFORE it starts; having a toolbox of mental health motivators can be the key to that.

Get Ready

Everything changes. It's as simple as that. If you're not shifting, changing, and growing, you're dying. Each step and choice we make in life is leading us somewhere. Whether it's toward our dream life or away from it. And remember, if it's away, you can always make the CHOICE to pivot your life into a new direction as well. Nothing is forever.

Change is scary. It just is. Humans like routines, patterns, control, and knowing what to expect. But there can be a lot of amazing things and anticipation in the pivot at well! These are our opportunities to take stock of what we've done in our lives up until now and see where we want it to go. With the right attitude, at any moment, at any time, in any pivot, you can change your entire life and start creating the dream life you've always wanted.

Not every change is by choice, and I get that, but with every change there is, for sure, opportunity. People don't hate change, they resist loss. Loss of what they thought their life would look like or what they wanted it to be. Loss of what was once considered "normal" and what was expected.

There's a lot of fear in change. We're afraid we won't know who we are if we change or, worse, what if people don't like us once we do? What if I show people the real me or work toward what I ACTUALLY want and I fail? The only failure in life is not trying. When you put yourself out there and go for it, one of two things happen: You're either super successful and it was all worth the risk! Or, it doesn't go the way you'd hoped, you learn a ton in the process, and it was all worth the risk. Resisting change and fearing loss doesn't actually provide you anything in life. You don't prevent change, you just keep making choices that drag out the process and take you away from the incredible human you were born to be! Fail forward!

If the change was something you didn't want and seems to have ruined your life, step back and see it from God's eyes. Is there something in this I can use? Is there part of this pain that can help me to grow and transform? Is this part of my story going to serve someone else who has also been through this? It's hard to be grateful for loss. But losing someone or something important to you means that you had it at one point and that's a beautiful thing. It also means you can have it again. As we change and shift in life, just because something looks different doesn't mean it's not just as beautiful. If you've lost a loved one, that love may re-enter your life in a different form. Or your story may help you to bond with someone and help them through their own grief.

If the change is a choice that you're making (going for a new career, moving, ending a relationship), first off, step back and give yourself a HUGE pat on the back. Stepping out and making a choice to pivot is one of the bravest things you can do in life. Especially if you're not happy in your current situation. The whole "something is better than nothing" attitude has kept many-a-people stuck in settling. You've made the decision to boldly declare, "I deserve more and I love myself enough to go claim it!" That's huge!

Now that you've taken the first big leap, you may find yourself in the, "Holy cow, this was WAY scarier than I expected it to be" moment. It's ok, that's pretty normal. Take a breath and go back to your WHY. Remembering why this change was so important in the first place is the key to staying on track. I left because I wasn't happy. I started my own business because I was sick of depending on others to give me my dream job. I moved because that place didn't fit with my lifestyle anymore. Don't let the fear of the leap cause you to run back up and hide under a rock. And don't let yourself off the hook with thinking, "Well, I tried it so I guess I went after my dreams." Trying something and realizing you don't love it after all is a different story. But remember WHY you wanted the change, and WHO you're working to become. Give it a solid chance and trust your gut with each move.

We only get a finite amount of time on this spinning globe so why not really go for it and live the kind of life you love? And if you realize 5, 10, 100 times along the way that that keeps changing, change along with it. Once you can learn to expect and embrace the changes that are happening in your life, life gets pretty exciting. You can learn to be kind to yourself and proud of yourself for your pivots. You can forgive and let go of who and what no longer serves you, and you can see each heart break as an opportunity to push you more into the life you ACTUALLY want.

Don't let the fear of what could POSSIBLY go wrong keep you from going after what you ACTUALLY want. Don't use past pivots that didn't work out so well to convince yourself that you don't deserve X or you can't risk Y. See yourself as your loved ones see you – and remember you're stronger and more capable than you give yourself credit for.

I used to take my dad's advice of, "Ask yourself, will this matter in two years?" to keep me from avoiding huge life changes because YES, YES IT WILL! But also ask yourself, "What will staying on this path look like in two years and do I like the way that it looks?" If the answer is no, don't keep spinning on the same hamster wheel. And who cares if you go big and it doesn't work out?

Again, no one cares about what you're doing as much as you think that they do. They're worried about their own crazy life decisions and changes and what you think of them, ironically enough. If we're all just in our own world, doing our own thing, why not go after the big things you want in life?

Map out the dream life you want (each time your life changes). Journal about it, create the vision board, speak it into freaking existence. Then, create a plan and work it backward to what goals you can work on today and routines you can create to get you into that dream life. Let go of what no longer serves you and seek out the biggest things that will. Lean into your faith and know that you're not doing this alone.

As I'm sitting here, in a completely empty apartment with nothing but my laptop and a camping chair, I find myself at another big ol' life pivot. I'm stepping into a new relationship, moving from Los Angeles to Denver amidst a global pandemic, I'm about to start a new job, creating a second travel channel, and writing this book.

To say I've learned to thrive in change is an understatement but that doesn't keep it from being any less scary. I just know that there truly is power in pivoting.

Harness it, go forth, and create the life of your dreams! You're a freaking rockstar!

"You are never too old to set another goal or to dream a new dream."

~ C.S. Lewis

Resources

I am a huge proponent of being a life-long learner and I love me some self-help books! If you're looking to dive into more of the incredibleness that's inside of you, check out some of my favorite books that have "pivoted" my own life and inspired so much of this book.

"You Are a Badass: How to Stop Doubting Your Greatness and Start Living an Awesome Life" by Jen Sincero

This book is EVERYTHING! This was the first self-help book that felt like just a good ol' girlfriend dropping some gems of knowledge to help me become a better person. Jen writes in a funny, light-hearted manner but her stories also cut me to the core. She poses all of the right big questions, helping readers to discover what they ACTUALLY want to be doing in their lives.

"Option B: Facing Adversity, Building Resilience, and Finding Joy" by Sheryl Sandberg

After losing her husband suddenly, Sheryl finds herself learning how to navigate through her grief and trauma. This book helped me to understand many of the emotions I was feeling post-divorce. She breaks it down in a relatable and understandable way by using her own personal journey of healing. This is an amazing book if you've experienced any sort of loss.

"The Alchemist" by Paulo Coelho

This is the ultimate book for anyone feeling lost in life and for those looking to find a path to forge their own journey. The book uses the fictional quest of an Andalusian Shepherd boy who's following his passion and dreams. This book is a guide full of insanely quotable goodness that helps to teach us how to listen to our own hearts and dream big.

"Everything Is Figureoutable" by Marie Forleo

Marie is a business and life guru who is freaking hilarious! I fell in love with her on her YouTube channel "Marie TV" where she breaks down life's biggest questions and lessons into funny, practical answers. Her book is one giant pile of knowledge on productivity and positivity.

"The Four Agreements" by Don Miguel Ruiz

This book makes it all so simple. 1. Be impeccable with your word. 2. Don't take anything personally. 3. Don't make assumptions. And 4.

Always do your best. I mean, I think those are four principles we can all get behind.

"Loving What Is" by Byron Katie

Byron Katie really breaks down the lies we tell ourselves and takes a no-bullshit approach to all of our negative self-talk. As I mentioned in Chapter 4, a big part of preserving our mental health comes from digging into what's ACTUALLY true in the statements we play in our brains. This book delves into this practice in more detail.

"Eat, Pray, Love: One Woman's Search for Everything Across Italy, India and Indonesia" by Elizabeth Gilbert

Pizza, wine, and overcoming trauma – what's not to love about this book? It's the ultimate divorce survival story of embracing your second chance. If you're looking for a book that will make you laugh and cry at the same time, this one's for you!

"You Are The One: A Bold Adventure in Finding Purpose, Discovering the Real You, and Loving Fully" by Kute Blackson

After my divorce I found myself dating...a LOT! A friend suggested this book as a way to step back, deal with the trauma and loss, and learn to love myself wholly without anyone else. This is the ultimate self-love guide with the perfect combination of woo-woo goodness and practical advice.

"The Universe Has Your Back: Transform Fear to Faith" by Gabrielle Bernstein

I felt this book SO hard! Gabby talks about how she had her life perfectly planned out until she eventually realized that things were not going to happen in her way or in her time, no matter how much she tried to force them to. She takes meditation and release to a whole new level and teaches us all how to lean into our faith and let go.

"#Girlboss" by Sophia Amoroso

Pivoting in your career? Go grab this book ASAP. Sophia is the ultimate role model of someone who leaned into the unexpected and carved out her own path. Her hilarious tales of being the outsider and turning her passions into a successful business will have you ready to take on your next endeavor with style!

"Failing Up: How to Take Risks, Aim Higher, and Never Stop Learning" by Leslie Odom Jr.

As a musical theater geek, I was into this one the second Leslie talked about his time in "Rent." But this author has SO many amazing lessons of failure, listening to your gut, and putting yourself out there by risking it all. Plus, I just love the whole notion of "failing up."

Acknowledgements

This was a book I never planned to write and I have so many people to thank for the creation of it. Gotta start off by giving props to my family. When most parents would have gently started trying to push their kids into "normal" jobs with "stability", mine have been rockstars raising two entrepreneurial, creative kids...aka broke kids. They've supported us through and through and never stopped believing we could turn our dreams into successes. Thank you to the friends (old and new) who have been by my side through the many "pivots" throughout the years. And to the ones who are no longer in my life, thank you for the seasons you were there and nothing but love left for ya! Thank you to the wonderful people who have helped me Google, scream, and cry through the process of learning how to create a book in the first place. And a special thank you to Steve, who showed up out of nowhere as the world was falling apart and helped my world fall into place. None of this would be possible without any of you!

About the Author

Monica Ortega is a professional on-camera host, speaker, and actress from Holt, Michigan. She created the online travel show *Monica Goes* in 2014 to inspire others to break out of their comfort zones and go on adventures. As someone who's afraid of everything, she'll put herself through almost anything to show that if an average everyday person like her can do these things, anyone can.

She has produced and hosted more than 100 episodes, created destination videos for over 40 DMO's, and been featured on Matador Network, USA Today's 10Best, Insider Travel, REI, and more!

Monica has spoken openly about how her personal setbacks have helped her pivot into creating a life that she loves. She speaks at events around the country helping others to embrace change and create their own dream life.

Monica emcees at some of the biggest music festivals in the nation and has been seen in over 20 commercials on TV. She is also the co-host of the podcast Stumblin' Forward which is all about the missteps of entrepreneurship.

When she's not traveling, Monica can usually be found line dancing, singing in cover bands, or out on a hiking trail with her adventure dog Millie exploring their new home in Denver, Colorado.

Made in the USA
Monee, IL
03 June 2021